THE YALE SHAKESPEARE

THE TEMPEST

Edited by David Horne

NEW HAVEN : YALE UNIVERSITY PRESS

London: Oxford University Press

Preface of the General Editors

AS the late Professor Tucker Brooke has observed, practically all modern editions of Shakespeare are 18th-century versions of the plays, based on the additions, alterations, and emendations of editors of that period. It has been our purpose, as it was Professor Brooke's, to give the modern reader Shakespeare's plays in the approximate form of their original appearance.

About half the plays appeared in quarto form before the publication of the First Folio in 1623. Thus for a large number of plays the only available text is that of the Folio. In the case of quarto plays our policy has been to use that text as the basis of the edition, unless it is clear that the text has been contaminated.

Interesting for us today is the fact that there are no act or scene divisions in the Quartos with the exception of *Othello*, which does mark Acts I, II, IV, and V but lacks indications of scenes. Even in the Folio, although act divisions are generally noted, only a part of the scenes are divided. In no case, either in Quarto or Folio, is there any indication of the place of action. The manifold scene divisions for the battle in such a play as *Antony and Cleopatra*, together with such locations as "Another part of the field," are the additions of the 18th century.

We have eliminated all indications of the place and time of action, because there is no authority for them in the originals and because Shakespeare gives such information, when it is requisite for understanding the play, through the dialogue of the actors. We have been sparing in our use of added scene and, in some cases, act divisions, because these frequently impede the flow of the action, which in Shakespeare's time was curiously like that of modern films.

Spelling has been modernized except when the original clearly indicates a pronunciation unlike our own, e.g. *desart* (desert), *divel* (devil), *banket* (banquet), and often in such Elizabethan syncopations as *ere* (e'er), *stolne* (stol'n), and *tane* (ta'en). In reproducing such forms we have followed the inconsistent usage of the original.

We have also preserved much more of the original capitalization than is usual, for often this is a part of the meaning. In like manner we have tended to adopt the lineation of the original in many cases where modern editors print prose as verse or verse as prose. We have, moreover, followed the original punctuation wherever it was practicable.

In verse we print a final *-ed* to indicate its full syllabic value, otherwise *'d*. In prose we have followed the inconsistencies of the original in this respect.

Our general practice has been to include in footnotes all information a reader needs for immediate understanding of the given page. In somewhat empiric fashion we repeat glosses as we think the reader needs to be reminded of the meaning. Further information is given in notes (indicated by the letter *N* in the footnotes) to be found at the back of each volume. Appendices deal with the text and sources of the play.

Square brackets indicate material not found in the original text. Long emendations or lines taken from another authoritative text of a play are indicated in the footnotes for the information of the reader. We have silently corrected obvious typographical errors.

CONTENTS

[THE ACTORS' NAMES]

The scene: [*A ship at sea and then*]
an uninhabited island

Names of the Actors

ALONSO, *K[ing] of Naples*
SEBASTIAN, *his brother*
PROSPERO, *the right Duke of Milan*
ANTONIO, *his brother, the usurping Duke of Milan*
FERDINAND, *son to the King of Naples*
GONZALO, *an honest old councilor*
ADRIAN *and* ⎱ *Lords*
FRANCISCO ⎰
CALIBAN, *a salvage and deformed slave*
TRINCULO, *a jester*
STEPHANO, *a drunken butler*
Master of a ship
Boatswain
Mariners

MIRANDA, *daughter to Prospero*
ARIEL, *an airy spirit*

IRIS
CERES
JUNO ⎱ *Spirits*
NYMPHS
REAPERS

[The Actors' Names] N. (N refers throughout to the correspond-
ing note given at the end of the text.) councilor F *councellor;*
see OED; N.

THE TEMPEST

Act I

SCENE 1

A tempestuous noise of thunder and lightning heard.
Enter a Shipmaster and a Boatswain.

Master. Boatswain!
Boatswain. Here, Master! What cheer?
Master. Good. Speak to th' mariners. Fall to't,
yarely, or we run ourselves aground—bestir, bestir!
                                                              Exit.

Enter Mariners.

Boatswain. Heigh, my hearts! Cheerly, cheerly, my
hearts! Yare, yare! Take in the topsail! Tend to th'
Master's whistle! Blow till thou burst thy wind, if
room enough!   8

Enter Alonso, Sebastian, Antonio, Ferdinand,
Gonzalo, and others.

Alonso. Good Boatswain, have care! Where's the
Master? Play the men!   10
Boatswain. I pray now, keep below.

Act I N. 2 **What cheer** what mood are you in (i.e. optimistic
or pessimistic)? 3 **Good** i.e. good cheer N. 4 **yarely** quickly. 7–8
Blow . . . enough N. 10 **Play the men** keep the men moving.

Antonio. Where is the Master, Boson?

Boatswain. Do you not hear him? You mar our labor. Keep your cabins—you do assist the storm.

Gonzalo. Nay, good, be patient.   15

Boatswain. When the sea is. Hence! What cares these roarers for the name of king? To cabin: silence! trouble us not!

Gonzalo. Good, yet remember whom thou hast aboard.   20

Boatswain. None that I more love than myself. You are a councilor. If you can command these elements to silence and work the peace of the present, we will not hand a rope more; use your authority. If you cannot, give thanks you have lived so long and make yourself ready in your cabin for the mischance of the hour, if it so hap. Cheerly, good hearts! Out of our way, I say.   *Exit.*

Gonzalo. I have great comfort from this fellow: methinks he hath no drowning mark upon him; his complexion is perfect gallows. Stand fast, good fate, to his hanging! Make the rope of his destiny our cable, for our own doth little advantage! If he be not born to be hanged, our case is miserable.   *Exeunt.*

Enter Boatswain.

---

12 **Boson** boatswain. 13 **hear him** i.e. hear his whistle; see l. 7 above. 15 **good** good fellow. 16 **cares** N. **roarers** waves (to roar was to bluster and boast as well as to shout). 22 **councilor** F *counsellor.* 27 **Cheerly . . . hearts** spoken to the crew. 29–31 **methinks . . . gallows** from an old proverb, 'He that's born to be hanged need fear no drowning.' 33 **doth . . . advantage** benefits us little.

2

Boatswain. Down with the topmast! yare, lower, lower! Bring her to try with main-course.   36

A cry within.

A plague upon this howling! They are louder than the weather or our office.

Enter Sebastian, Antonio, and Gonzalo.

Yet again? What do you here? Shall we give ore and drown? Have you a mind to sink?   40

Sebastian. A pox o' your throat, you bawling, blasphemous, incharitable dog!

Boatswain. Work you, then.

Antonio. Hang, cur, hang, you whoreson, insolent noisemaker; we are less afraid to be drown'd than thou art.   46

Gonzalo. I'll warrant him for drowning, though the ship were no stronger than a nutshell and as leaky as an unstanched wench.   49

Boatswain. Lay her ahold, ahold! Set her two courses off to sea again; lay her off!

Enter Mariners, wet.

Mariners. All lost! To prayers, to prayers, all lost!

[*Exeunt Mariners.*]

Boatswain. What, must our mouths be cold?

Gonzalo. The king and prince at prayers! Let's assist them, for our case is as theirs.   55

Sebastian. I am out of patience.

Antonio. We are merely cheated of our lives by

35 **Down** . . . **topmast** N. 36 **main-course** mainsail. 47 **warrant** . . . **drowning** be his guarantee against drowning. 50 **ahold** so as to hold the wind N. 51 **courses** sails. 52–66 N. 53 **must** . . . **cold** N. 57 **merely** utterly, without qualification (cf. *Hamlet*, I.2.137; *As You Like It*, II.7.140).

3

drunkards. This wide-chopp'd rascal, would thou might'st lie drowning the washing of ten tides.   59

Gonzalo. He'll be hanged yet, though every drop of water swear against it and gape at wid'st to glut him.

[*Exit Boatswain.*]

A confused noise within.

[*Voices.*] 'Mercy on us!' 'We split, we split!' 'Farewell, my wife and children; farewell, brother!' 'We split! we split! we split!'

Antonio. Let's all sink with' king.   65

Sebastian. Let's take leave of him.

[*Exeunt Sebastian and Antonio.*]

Gonzalo. Now would I give a thousand furlongs of sea for an acre of barren ground: long heath, brown furze, anything. The wills above be done, but I would fain die a dry death.   *Exit.*

SCENE 2

Enter Prospero and Miranda.

Miranda. If by your art, my dearest father, you have
Put the wild waters in this roar, allay them.
The sky it seems would pour down stinking pitch,
But that the sea, mounting to th' welkin's cheek,
Dashes the fire out. O! I have suffered   5
With those that I saw suffer: a brave vessel—

58 **wide-chopp'd** big-mouthed. 59 **washing . . . tides** N. 61 **glut** gulp. 68–9 **heath . . . furze** shrubs found growing on wasteland. 4 **welkin's** sky's. 5 **fire** here disyllabic. 6 **brave** here, as elsewhere in the play, 'admirable.'

4

Who had no doubt some noble creature in her—
Dash'd all to pieces. O the cry did knock
Against my very heart. Poor souls, they perish'd.
Had I bin any god of power, I would   10
Have sunk the sea within the earth, or ere
It should the good ship so have swallow'd, and
The fraughting souls within her.

   Prospero.   Be collected:
No more amazement. Tell your piteous heart   14
There's no harm done.

   Miranda.   O woe the day!

   Prospero.   No harm.
I have done nothing but in care of thee—
Of thee my dear one, thee my daughter—who
Art ignorant of what thou art, nought knowing
Of whence I am, nor that I am more better
Than Prospero, master of a full poor cell,   20
And thy no greater father.

   Miranda.   More to know
Did never meddle with my thoughts.

   Prospero.   'Tis time
I should inform thee farther: Lend thy hand
And pluck my magic garment from me. So,
Lie there, my art. Wipe thou thine eyes; have com-
    fort;   25
The direful spectacle of the wrack which touch'd
The very virtue of compassion in thee
I have with such provision in mine art
So safely order'd that there is no soil,

11 **or ere** before. 13 **fraughting souls** souls who composed her
freight. 14 **amazement** astonished terror. **piteous** full of pity.
19 **more better** N. 20 **full** very. 24 **magic garment** N. 27 **virtue**
essence. 28 **provision** foresight. 29 **soil** N.

No, not so much perdition as an hair,   30
Betid to any creature in the vessel
Which thou heard'st cry, which thou saw'st sink. Sit
    down,
For thou must now know farther.
  Miranda.   You have often
Begun to tell me what I am, but stopp'd
And left me to a bootless inquisition,   35
Concluding, 'Stay, not yet.'
  Prospero.   The hour's now come;
The very minute bids thee ope thine ear.
Obey and be attentive. Canst thou remember
A time before we came unto this cell?
I do not think thou canst, for then thou wast not   40
Out three years old.
  Miranda.   Certainly, sir, I can.
  Prospero. By what? By any other house, or person?
Of anything the image tell me, that
Hath kept with thy remembrance.
  Miranda.   'Tis far off,
And rather like a dream than an assurance   45
That my remembrance warrants. Had I not
Four or five women once that tended me?
  Prospero. Thou hadst, and more, Miranda; but how
    is it
That this lives in thy mind? What seest thou else
In the dark backward and abysm of time?   50
If thou rememb'rest aught ere thou cam'st here,
How thou cam'st here thou mayst.
  Miranda.   But that I do not.
  Prospero. Twelve year since, Miranda, twelve year
    since,

30 **perdition** destruction. **hair** N. 35 **bootless inquisition** fruitless
inquiry. 41 **Out** quite, fully. 50 **backward** past. 53 **year . . .
year** the first *year* may be dissyllabic.

  6

Thy father was the Duke of Milan and
A prince of power.

    Miranda.   Sir, are not you my father?   55

    Prospero. Thy mother was a piece of virtue and
She said thou wast my daughter—and thy father
Was Duke of Milan—and his only heir
And princess, no worse issued.

    Miranda.   O the heavens,   59
What foul play had we that we came from thence?
Or blessed was't we did?

    Prospero.   Both, both, my girl.
By foul play, as thou sayst, were we heav'd thence,
But blessedly holp hither.

    Miranda.   O my heart bleeds
To think o' th' teen that I have turn'd you to,   64
Which is from my remembrance; please you, further.

    Prospero. My brother and thy uncle, call'd An-
    tonio—
I pray thee mark me, that a brother should
Be so perfidious—he whom next thyself
Of all the world I lov'd, and to him put
The manage of my state, as at that time   70
Through all the signories it was the first,
And Prospero the prime duke, being so reputed
In dignity, and for the liberal arts
Without a parallel, those being all my study—
The government I cast upon my brother,   75
And to my state grew stranger, being transported
And rapt in secret studies; thy false uncle—
Dost thou attend me?

---

54 **Milan** stressed $\smile \!\!' —$. 56 **piece** masterpiece. 59 **And princess** N.
63 **holp** helped. 64 **teen** trouble. 65 **from** out of. 71 **signories**
dukedoms. 72 **being** probably monosyllabic, as in ll. 74, 76.
77 **secret** i.e. magical.

Miranda.   Sir, most heedfully.
Prospero. Being once perfected how to grant suits,
How to deny them, who t' advance, and who   80
To trash for overtopping, new created
The creatures that were mine, I say, or chang'd 'em,
Or else new form'd 'em, having both the key
Of officer and office, set all hearts i' th' state
To what tune pleas'd his ear, that now he was   85
The ivy which had hid my princely trunk,
And suck'd my verdure out on't—thou attend'st not?
  Miranda. O good sir, I do.
  Prospero.   I pray thee, mark me:
I, thus neglecting worldly ends, all dedicated
To closeness and the bettering of my mind   90
With that which but by being so retired
Orepriz'd all popular rate, in my false brother
Awak'd an evil nature, and my trust,
Like a good parent, did beget of him
A falsehood, in its contrary as great   95
As my trust was, which had indeed no limit,
A confidence sans bound. He, being thus, lorded,
Not only with what my revenue yielded,
But what my power might else exact. Like one
Who having into truth by telling of it   100
Made such a sinner of his memory
To credit his own lie, he did believe
He was indeed the duke, out o' th' substitution,
And executing th' outward face of royalty   104

---

79 **perfected** stressed $\underline{\prime}$ — —. 81 **trash for overtopping** N. 83 **key**
play on 'musical key' and 'key for lock' (cf. present-day 'keys of
office'). 85 **that** so that. 87 **on't** of it. 90 **closeness** privacy. 91–2
With . . . rate N. 97 **lorded** ruled like a lord, domineered N.
98 **revenue** stressed — $\underline{\prime}$ —. 99–102 **Like . . . lie** N.

With all prerogative—hence, his ambition growing—
Dost thou hear?

  Miranda.   Your tale, sir, would cure deafness.

  Prospero. To have no screen between this part he
    play'd
And him he play'd it for, he needs will be
Absolute Milan. Me, poor man, my library   109
Was dukedom large enough; of temporal royalties
He thinks me now incapable, confederates—
So dry he was for sway—wi' th' King of Naples
To give him annual tribute, do him homage,
Subject his coronet to his crown and bend   114
The dukedom, yet unbow'd—alas, poor Milan—
To most ignoble stooping.

  Miranda.   O the heavens!

  Prospero. Mark his condition and th' event, then
    tell me
If this might be a brother.

  Miranda.   I should sin
To think but nobly of my grandmother.   119
Good wombs have borne bad sons.

  Prospero.   Now the condition.
This King of Naples being an enemy
To me inveterate hearkens my brother's suit,
Which was that he in lieu o' th' premises
Of homage and I know not how much tribute
Should presently extirpate me and mine   125
Out of the dukedom and confer fair Milan,

109 **Absolute Milan** Duke of Milan. **Me** as for me. 110 **temporal
royalties** worldly attributes of kingship. 111 **confederates** con-
spires. 112 **dry** thirsty. **sway** rule. **wi' th'** F *with.* 117 **condition** the
condition of his bargain with Naples (ll. 123–6). 119 **but** otherwise than. 123 **in lieu o'** in consideration of. **premises** conditions.
125 **presently** at once. **extirpate** stressed — ´ —.

With all the honors, on my brother; whereon,
A treacherous army levied, one midnight
Fated to th' purpose did Antonio open
The gates of Milan, and i' th' dead of darkness   130
The ministers for th' purpose hurried thence
Me and thy crying self.

   Miranda.   Alack, for pity!
I not rememb'ring how I cried out then
Will cry it ore again—it is a hint
That wrings mine eyes to't.

   Prospero.   Hear a little further, 135
And then I'll bring thee to the present business
Which now's upon's, without the which this story
Were most impertinent.

   Miranda.   Wherefore did they not
That hour destroy us?

   Prospero.   Well demanded, wench.   139
My tale provokes that question. Dear, they durst not,
So dear the love my people bore me, nor set
A mark so bloody on the business, but
With colors fairer painted their foul ends.
In few, they hurried us aboard a bark,   144
Bore us some leagues to sea, where they prepar'd
A rotten carcass of a butt, not rigg'd,
Nor tackle, sail, nor mast; the very rats
Instinctively have quit it. There they hoist us,
To cry to th' sea that roar'd to us, to sigh
To th' winds whose pity, sighing back again,   150
Did us but loving wrong.

131 **ministers** agents. 134 **hint** occasion. 138 **impertinent** not pertinent, out of place. 139 **demanded** asked. **wench** young woman. 144 **In few** in few words. 146 **carcass of a butt** derelict ship (with *butt*—'a cask for wine'—cf. present-day derogatory 'tub'). 148 **hoist** originally the past tense of 'hoise,' to raise with block and tackle. 151 **loving wrong** oxymoron.

Miranda.   Alack, what trouble
Was I then to you!
  Prospero.   O, a cherubin
Thou wast that did preserve me; thou didst smile,
Infused with a fortitude from heaven,
When I have deck'd the sea with drops full salt,   155
Under my burthen groan'd, which rais'd in me
An undergoing stomach, to bear up
Against what should ensue.
  Miranda.   How came we ashore?
  Prospero. By providence divine.
Some food we had, and some fresh water, that   160
A noble Neapolitan, Gonzalo,
Out of his charity—who being then appointed
Master of this design—did give us, with
Rich garments, linens, stuffs, and necessaries   164
Which since have steaded much; so of his gentleness,
Knowing I lov'd my books, he furnish'd me
From mine own library with volumes that
I prize above my dukedom.
  Miranda.   Would I might
But ever see that man!
  Prospero.   Now I arise:
Sit still and hear the last of our sea-sorrow.   170
Here in this island we arriv'd, and here
Have I, thy schoolmaster, made thee more profit
Than other princess can, that have more time
For vainer hours and tutors not so careful.
  Miranda. Heavens thank you for't! And now I pray
      you, sir—   175

157 **undergoing stomach** enduring courage. 165 **steaded much**
cf. the modern 'stood in good stead.' 169 **Now I arise** N. 172 **made
thee more profit** made thee profit more, i.e. better educated.
173 **princess** N.

11

For still 'tis beating in my mind—your reason
For raising this sea storm?
  Prospero.   Know thus far forth:
By accident most strange, bountiful fortune—
Now my dear lady—hath mine enemies
Brought to this shore; and by my prescience   180
I find my zenith doth depend upon
A most auspicious star, whose influence
If now I court not but omit, my fortunes
Will ever after droop—here cease more questions.
Thou art inclin'd to sleep; 'tis a good dullness,   185
And give it way—I know thou canst not choose.
Come away, servant, come! I am ready now.
Approach, my Ariel. Come!

Enter Ariel.

  Ariel. All hail, great master, grave sir, hail! I come
To answer thy best pleasure, be't to fly,   190
To swim, to dive into the fire, to ride
On the curl'd clouds: to thy strong bidding task
Ariel and all his quality.
  Prospero.   Hast thou, spirit,
Perform'd to point the tempest that I bade thee?
  Ariel. To every article.   195
I boarded the king's ship; now on the beak,
Now in the waist, the deck, in every cabin
I flam'd amazement; sometime I'ld divide

179 **Now my dear lady** refers to fortune. 181–2 N. 185 **dullness**
drowsiness. 186 **give it way** do not fight it. **canst not choose** N.
187 **Come away** i.e. from where you are to here. 192 **task** put to
the test. 193 **all his quality** 'all others of his profession,' i.e. the
other spirits 194 **to point** in every point, exactly. 198 **flam'd
amazement** caused amazement by my flames.

   12

And burn in many places; on the topmast,   199
The yards and boresprit would I flame distinctly,
Then meet and join. Jove's lightning, the precursors
O' th' dreadful thunderclaps, more momentary
And sight-outrunning were not; the fire and cracks
Of sulphurous roaring the most mighty Neptune
Seem to besiege, and make his bold waves tremble,
Yea, his dread trident shake.

  Prospero.   My brave spirit!   206
Who was so firm, so constant, that this coil
Would not infect his reason?

  Ariel.   Not a soul
But felt a fever of the mad, and play'd
Some tricks of desperation; all but mariners   210
Plung'd in the foaming brine and quit the vessel.
Then all afire with me the king's son, Ferdinand,
With hair up-staring—then like reeds, not hair—
Was the first man that leapt, cried 'Hell is empty,
And all the divels are here!'

  Prospero.   Why, that's my spirit!
But was not this nigh shore?

  Ariel.   Close by, my master.

  Prospero. But are they, Ariel, safe?

  Ariel.   Not a hair
      perish'd: 217
On their sustaining garments not a blemish,
But fresher than before; and as thou bad'st me,
In troops I have dispers'd them 'bout the isle.   220
The king's son have I landed by himself,

200 **boresprit** bowsprit; the reference is to St. Elmo's fire. **distinctly** separately. 205 **Seem** to seem'd to (with -*d* and *t*- merged). 207 **coil** turmoil. 209 **fever of the mad** fit of irrationality. 213 **up-staring** standing on end. 218. **sustaining** 'buoyant,' probably through Ariel's magic.

Whom I left cooling of the air with sighs,
In an odd angle of the isle, and sitting,
His arms in this sad knot.

Prospero.   Of the king's ship,
The mariners, say how thou hast dispos'd,   225
And all the rest o' th' fleet.

Ariel.   Safely in harbor
Is the king's ship, in the deep nook where once
Thou call'dst me up at midnight to fetch dew
From the still-vex'd Bermoothes; there she's hid,
The mariners all under hatches stow'd,   230
Who with a charm join'd to their suff'red labor
I have left asleep; and for the rest o' th' fleet—
Which I dispers'd—they all have met again
And are upon the Mediterranean flote
Bound sadly home for Naples,   235
Supposing that they saw the king's ship wrack'd,
And his great person perish.

Prospero.   Ariel, thy charge
Exactly is perform'd; but there's more work.
What is the time o' th' day?

Ariel.   Past the mid season.

Prospero. At least two glasses. The time 'twixt six
and now   240
Must by us both be spent most preciously.

Ariel. Is there more toil? Since thou dost give me
pains,
Let me remember thee what thou hast promis'd,
Which is not yet perform'd me.

---

229 still-vex'd **Bermoothes** (three syllables) ever-stormy Bermudas N. 234 **flote** wave, billows. 240 **glasses** hourglasses. 242 **pains** trouble in accomplishing tasks (cf. present-day 'painstaking'). 243 **remember** remind.

14

Prospero. How now? moody?
What is't thou canst demand?

Ariel. My liberty. 245

Prospero. Before the time be out? No more!

Ariel. I prithee
Remember I have done thee worthy service,
Told thee no lies, made thee no mistakings, serv'd
Without or grudge or grumblings; thou didst promise
To bate me a full year.

Prospero. Dost thou forget 250
From what a torment I did free thee?

Ariel. No.

Prospero. Thou dost, and think'st it much to tread
the ooze
Of the salt deep,
To run upon the sharp wind of the North,
To do me business in the veins o' th' earth 255
When it is bak'd with frost.

Ariel. I do not, sir.

Prospero. Thou liest, malignant thing! Hast thou
forgot
The foul witch Sycorax, who with age and envy
Was grown into a hoop? Hast thou forgot her? 259

Ariel. No, sir.

Prospero. Thou hast. Where was she born?
Speak! Tell me!

Ariel. Sir, in Argier.

Prospero. Oh, was she so! I must
Once in a month recount what thou hast bin,
Which thou forget'st. This damn'd witch Sycorax,
For mischiefs manifold and sorceries terrible

248 **Told thee . . . made thee** N. 249 **or . . . or** either . . . or,
didst F *did.* 250 **bate me** reduce my service by. 256 **bak'd** hardened. 261 **Argier** Algiers.

15

To enter human hearing, from Argier   265
Thou know'st was banish'd; for one thing she did
They would not take her life. Is not this true?
   Ariel. Ay, sir.
   Prospero. This blue-ey'd hag was hither brought
     with child,
And here was left by th' sailors; thou, my slave,   270
As thou report'st thyself, was then her servant,
And for thou wast a spirit too delicate
To act her earthy and abhorr'd commands,
Refusing her grand hests, she did confine thee
By help of her more potent ministers,   275
And in her most unmitigable rage,
Into a cloven pine, within which rift
Imprison'd thou didst painfully remain
A dozen years; within which space she died
And left thee there, where thou didst vent thy
     groans   280
As fast as mill wheels strike. Then was this island—
Save for the son that she did litter here—
A freckled whelp, hag-born—not honor'd with
A human shape.
   Ariel.   Yes, Caliban her son.
   Prospero. Dull thing, I say so: he, that Caliban   285
Whom now I keep in service. Thou best know'st
What torment I did find thee in; thy groans
Did make wolves howl, and penetrate the breasts
Of ever-angry bears: it was a torment
To lay upon the damn'd, which Sycorax   290
Could not again undo; it was mine art,
When I arriv'd and heard thee, that made gape

266 **for one thing** perhaps 'because of one good thing' 269 **blue-ey'd** N. 272 **for** because. **spirit** one syllable (probably 'sprite').
273 **earthy** N. 274 **hests** commands. 281 **mill wheels strike** i.e.
the water. 282 **she** F *he.*

The pine and let thee out.

Ariel.   I thank thee, master.

Prospero. If thou more murmur'st, I will rend an oak

And peg thee in his knotty entrails till   295

Thou hast howl'd away twelve winters.

Ariel.   Pardon, master;

I will be correspondent to command

And do my spriting, gently.

Prospero. Do so, and after two days I will discharge thee.

Ariel. That's my noble master!   300

What shall I do? Say what! What shall I do?

Prospero. Go make thyself like a nymph o' th' sea; be subject

To no sight but thine and mine, invisible

To every eyeball else. Go take this shape

And hither come in't. Go! Hence with diligence!   305

                    Exit [Ariel].

Awake, dear heart, awake; thou hast slept well;

Awake.

Miranda.   The strangeness of your story put

Heaviness in me.

Prospero.   Shake it off! Come on,

We'll visit Caliban, my slave, who never

Yields us kind answer.

Miranda.   'Tis a villain, sir,   310

I do not love to look on.

Prospero.   But as 'tis

We cannot miss him; he does make our fire,

Fetch in our wood, and serves in offices

That profit us. What ho! slave! Caliban!   314

Thou earth, thou! speak!

297 **correspondent** submissive. 312 **miss** spare.

17

Caliban within.　　　　There's wood enough within.
Prospero. Come forth, I say, there's other business
　　for thee!
Come, thou tortoise! When?

Enter Ariel like a water nymph.

Fine apparition! My quaint Ariel,　　　　　　318
Hark in thine ear.
　Ariel.　　　　My lord, it shall be done.　*Exit.*
Prospero. Thou poisonous slave, got by the divel
　　himself
Upon thy wicked dam, come forth.

Enter Caliban.

　Caliban. As wicked dew as ere my mother brush'd
With raven's feather from unwholesome fen
Drop on you both! A southwest blow on ye,
And blister you all ore!　　　　　　　　　325
　Prospero. For this be sure tonight thou shalt have
　　cramps,
Side stitches, that shall pen thy breath up; urchins
Shall for that vast of night that they may work
All exercise on thee! Thou shalt be pinch'd
As thick as honeycomb, each pinch more stinging　330
Than bees that made 'em.
　Caliban.　　　　I must eat my dinner.
This island's mine by Sycorax my mother,
Which thou tak'st from me! When thou camest first

318 **quaint** finely dressed. 320 **got** begot. 324 **southwest** a southwest wind was considered infectious. 327 **urchins** goblins in the
shape of hedgehogs (cf. below, II.2.10–12). 328 **vast** immense
space. 329 **pinch'd** tormented (perhaps pricked with hedgehog
quills). 331 **'em** i.e. the (cells of) honeycomb. 333 **camest** F
cam'st.

Thou strok'st me, and made much of me; wouldst
    give me
Water with berries in't, and teach me how   335
To name the bigger light and how the less,
That burn by day and night; and then I lov'd thee
And show'd thee all the qualities o' th' isle,
The fresh springs, brine pits, barren place and fertile.
Curs'd be I that did so! All the charms   340
Of Sycorax—toads, beetles, bats—light on you!
For I am all the subjects that you have,
Which first was mine own king, and here you sty me
In this hard rock, whiles you do keep from me
The rest o' th' island.

  Prospero.   Thou most lying slave,   345
Whom stripes may move, not kindness! I have us'd
    thee—
Filth as thou art—with human care and lodg'd thee
In mine own cell, till thou didst seek to violate
The honor of my child.

  Caliban. O ho! O ho! would't had been done!   350
Thou didst prevent me; I had peopl'd else
This isle with Calibans.

  Miranda.   Abhorred slave,
Which any print of goodness wilt not take,

334 **strok'st** strok'dst; F *stroakst* N. 336 **bigger . . . less** see
Gen. 1:16: 'And God made two great lights; the greater light to
rule the day, and the lesser light to rule the night.' 339 **springs
. . . fertile** i.e. he showed how to distinguish between useful and
useless natural resources (Arden ed.). **place** N. 340 **charms** evil
spirits charmed by Sycorax. 343 **mine** F *min;* if not a printer's
error, the spelling may indicate a pronunciation, with *i* as in
'tin.' **sty me** pen me as in a pigsty. 352–63 N. 353 **Which . . . take**
who will not take any print (impression).

Being capable of all ill: I pitied thee,   354
Took pains to make thee speak, taught thee each hour
One thing or other; when thou didst not, savage,
Know thine own meaning, but wouldst gabble like
A thing most brutish, I endow'd thy purposes
With words that made them known, but thy vild
    race—
Though thou didst learn—had that in't which good
    natures
                          360
Could not abide to be with; therefore wast thou
Deservedly confin'd into this rock,
Who hadst deserv'd more than a prison.
   Caliban. You taught me language and my profit on't
Is, I know how to curse! The red plague rid you   365
For learning me your language!
   Prospero.   Hag-seed, hence!
Fetch us in fuel, and be quick thou'rt best
To answer other business! Shrug'st thou, malice?
If thou neglect'st or dost unwillingly
What I command, I'll rack thee with old cramps,   370
Fill all thy bones with aches, make thee roar
That beasts shall tremble at thy din.
   Caliban.   No, 'pray thee!
I must obey; his art is of such power
It would control my dam's god Setebos,
And make a vassal of him.
   Prospero.   So, slave, hence!   375
                                 Exit Caliban.

---

359 vild common spelling (showing pronunciation) of 'vile.'
360 good natures those who are naturally good. **365 red plague**
bubonic plague (with red sores). **rid** destroy. **367 be quick thou'rt
best** you had better be quick. **thou'rt** thou wert. **368 answer**
attend to. **371 aches** pronounced 'aitches.'
   20

*Enter Ferdinand; and Ariel, invisible, playing
and singing.*

Song

Ariel.   Come unto these yellow sands,
    and then take hands:
Curtsied when you have, and kiss'd,
    the wild waves whist,
Foot it featly here and there,   380
    And sweet sprites the burthen bear.

Burthen, dispersedly.

[Voices.] 'Hark, hark!' 'bowgh wawgh!'
    'The watch-dogs bark!' 'bowgh wawgh!'
Ariel.   Hark, hark! I hear
    The strain of strutting chanticleer   385
    Cry cockadiddle-dow!

Ferdinand. Where should this music be? i' th' air, or
    th' earth?
It sounds no more! And sure it waits upon
Some god o' th' island; sitting on a bank,
Weeping again the king my father's wrack,   390
This music crept by me upon the waters,
Allaying both their fury and my passion
With its sweet air; thence I have follow'd it—
Or it hath drawn me rather—but 'tis gone.
No, it begins again.   395

Song

Ariel.   Full fadom five thy father lies;
    Of his bones are coral made;

376–86 N. 379 **whist** hushed. 380 **featly** gracefully. 381 **the
burthen bear** F prints 'bear the burthen.' SD **Burthen, dispersedly** refrain, sung from several places on (or just off) the
stage. (SD is used throughout to indicate stage direction.) 390
Weeping again while I was weeping again because of. 392 **passion**
suffering. 396 **fadom** fathoms.

> Those are pearls that were his eyes:
> Nothing of him that doth fade,
> But doth suffer a sea change   400
> Into something rich and strange.
> Sea nymphs hourly ring his knell.

Burthen.

[Voices.] Ding dong!

[Ariel.]   Hark, now I hear them! Ding-dong, bell.

Ferdinand. The ditty does remember my drown'd
　　father.   405
This is no mortal business, nor no sound
That the earth owes! I hear it now above me.
　　Prospero. The fringed curtains of thine eye advance,
And say what thou seest yond.
　　Miranda.　　　　　　　　What is't? a spirit?
Lord, how it looks about! Believe me, sir,   410
It carries a brave form. But 'tis a spirit.
　　Prospero. No, wench, it eats and sleeps and hath
　　such senses
As we have, such. This gallant which thou seest
Was in the wrack; and but he's something stain'd
With grief—that's beauty's canker—thou might'st
　　call him   415
A goodly person. He has lost his fellows
And strays about to find 'em.
　　Miranda.　　　　　　　　I might call him
A thing divine, for nothing natural
I ever saw so noble.

405 **remember** recall. 407 **owes** possesses. 411 **brave** admirable.
414 **and but** except that. **something** somewhat. 415 **that's . . .
canker** which is the blight that destroys beauty. 416 **goodly**
handsome.

22

Prospero.   It goes on, I see,   419
As my soul prompts it! Spirit, fine spirit, I'll free thee
Within two days for this.
     Ferdinand.   Most sure the goddess
On whom these airs attend! Vouchsafe my prayer
May know if you remain upon this island,
And that you will some good instruction give
How I may bear me here! My prime request—   425
Which I do last pronounce—is—O you wonder!—
If you be maid or no?
     Miranda.   No wonder, sir,
But certainly a maid.
     Ferdinand.   My language? Heavens!
I am the best of them that speak this speech
Were I but where 'tis spoken.
     Prospero.   How? the best?   430
What wert thou if the King of Naples heard thee?
     Ferdinand. A single thing, as I am now, that won-
               ders
To hear thee speak of Naples! He does hear me,
And that he does, I weep. Myself am Naples,
Who with mine eyes—never since at ebb—beheld
The king my father wrack'd.
     Miranda.   Alack, for mercy!   436
     Ferdinand. Yes, faith, and all his lords, the Duke of
               Milan
And his brave son being twain.
     Prospero. [*Aside.*]   The Duke of Milan

420 Spirit . . . spirit both to be read 'sprite.' 423 remain dwell.
425 bear me conduct myself. 427 maid suggests two pairs of
opposites: goddess—mortal, unmarried—married. 432 single sol-
itary, alone, defenseless. 434 that because. 438 his brave son N.
                                        23

And his more braver daughter could control thee
If now 'twere fit to do't. At the first sight   440
They have chang'd eyes! Delicate Ariel,
I'll set thee free for this. —A word, good sir;
I fear you have done yourself some wrong! A word.
  Miranda. Why speaks my father so ungently? This
Is the third man that ere I saw! The first   445
That ere I sigh'd for! Pity move my father
To be inclin'd my way.
  Ferdinand.   O, if a virgin,
And your affection not gone forth, I'll make you
The Queen of Naples.
  Prospero.   Soft, sir. One word more.
[*Aside.*] They are both in either's powers! But this
    swift business   450
I must uneasy make, lest too light winning
Make the prize light. —One word more! I charge thee
That thou attend me! Thou dost here usurp
The name thou ow'st not and hast put thyself
Upon this island as a spy, to win it   455
From me, the lord on't.
  Ferdinand.   No, as I am a man.
  Miranda. There's nothing ill can dwell in such a
    temple.
If the ill spirit have so fair a house,
Good things will strive to dwell with't.
  Prospero.   Follow me.
Speak not you for him! He's a traitor! Come,   460
I'll manacle thy neck and feet together!
Sea water shalt thou drink; thy food shall be
The fresh brook mussels, wither'd roots, and husks

439 **control thee** check your statement, hence refute. 441 **chang'd**
play on 'exchanged' and 'altered.' 443 **done . . . wrong** euphemism for 'lied.' 451–2 **light . . . light** play on meanings 'easy'
and 'of small account.' 454 **ow'st** own'st.

Wherein the acorn cradled. Follow.

Ferdinand.   No,
I will resist such entertainment till   465
Mine enemy has more power.

                    He draws, and is charmed from moving.

Miranda.   O dear father,
Make not too rash a trial of him, for
He's gentle and not fearful.

Prospero.   What, I say!
My foot my tutor? Put thy sword up, traitor,
Who mak'st a show, but dar'st not strike, thy con-
       science   470
Is so possess'd with guilt! Come, from thy ward,
For I can here disarm thee with this stick,
And make thy weapon drop.

Miranda.   Beseech you, Father!

Prospero. Hence! Hang not on my garments.

Miranda.   Sir,
       have pity!
I'll be his surety.

Prospero.   Silence! One word more   475
Shall make me chide thee, if not hate thee! What,
An advocate for an impostor? Hush!
Thou think'st there is no more such shapes as he,
Having seen but him and Caliban! Foolish wench,
To th' most of men this is a Caliban,   480
And they to him are angels.

Miranda.   My affections
Are then most humble: I have no ambition
To see a goodlier man.

Prospero.   Come on, obey!

---

465 entertainment treatment. 468 **gentle** a gentleman. **fearful**
afraid. 469 **My . . . tutor** N. 471 **from thy ward** lower thy guard.
480–1 **To . . .** to compared to. 481 **affections** feelings.

Thy nerves are in their infancy again,
And have no vigor in them.

Ferdinand. So they are. 485
My spirits, as in a dream, are all bound up:
My father's loss, the weakness which I feel,
The wrack of all my friends, nor this man's threats,
To whom I am subdu'd, are but light to me,
Might I but through my prison once a day 490
Behold this maid! All corners else o' th' earth
Let liberty make use of: space enough
Have I in such a prison.

Prospero. [*To Ariel.*] It works! [*To Ferdinand.*]
Come on.
[*To Ariel.*] Thou hast done well, fine Ariel! [*To Ferdinand.*] Follow me.
[*To Ariel.*] Hark what thou else shalt do me.

Miranda. Be of
comfort.
My father's of a better nature, sir, 496
Than he appears by speech: this is unwonted
Which now came from him.

Prospero. Thou shalt be as free
As mountain winds; but then exactly do
All points of my command.

Ariel. To th' syllable. 500

Prospero. [*To Ferdinand.*] Come, follow! [*To Miranda.*] Speak not for him. *Exeunt.*

484 **nerves** sinews. 486 **spirits** vital powers.

Act II

SCENE 1

Enter Alonso, Sebastian, Antonio, Gonzalo, Adrian,
Francisco, and others.

Gonzalo. Beseech you, sir, be merry; you have
    cause—
So have we all—of joy, for our escape
Is much beyond our loss; our hint of woe
Is common: every day some sailor's wife,
The masters of some merchant, and the merchant   5
Have just our theme of woe. But for the miracle—
I mean our preservation—few in millions
Can speak like us! Then wisely, good sir, weigh
Our sorrow with our comfort.
  Alonso.   Prithee, peace.
  Sebastian. He receives comfort like cold porridge. 10
  Antonio. The visitor will not give him ore so.
  Sebastian. Look, he's winding up the watch of his
wit. By and by it will strike.
  Gonzalo. Sir—
  Sebastian. One! Tell.   15
  Gonzalo. When every grief is entertain'd that's of-
fer'd, comes to th' entertainer—
  Sebastian. A dollar.

3 **hint** occasion. 5 **some merchant** either a vessel or the owner
(or purchaser) of cargo. **the merchant** here, probably, in the latter sense. 10 **porridge** a stew, often with peas; cf. *peace* in l. 9
(Arden ed.). 11 **visitor** comforter of the sick (cf. below, ll. 199–200,
and Mat. 25:36). 13 **By and by** immediately. 15 **Tell** count.
16–20 N.

27

Gonzalo. Dolour comes to him indeed. You have spoken truer than you purpos'd. 20

Sebastian. You have taken it wiselier than I meant you should.

Gonzalo. Therefore, my lord—

Antonio. Fie, what a spendthrift is he of his tongue.

Alonso. I prithee spare. 25

Gonzalo. Well, I have done. But yet—

Sebastian. He will be talking.

Antonio. Which, of he or Adrian, for a good wager, first begins to crow?

Sebastian. The old cock. 30

Antonio. The cock'rel.

Sebastian. Done! The wager?

Antonio. A laughter.

Sebastian. A match.

Adrian. Though this island seem to be desert— 35

Sebastian. Ha ha ha!

Antonio. So! You're paid.

Adrian. Uninhabitable and almost inaccessible—

Sebastian. Yet—

Adrian. Yet— 40

Antonio. He could not miss't.

Adrian. It must needs be of subtle, tender, and delicate temperance.

Antonio. Temperance was a delicate wench. 44

Sebastian. Ay, and a subtle, as he most learnedly deliver'd.

Adrian. The air breathes upon us here most sweetly.

Sebastian. As if it had lungs, and rotten ones.

25 **spare** spare me any more talk. 33 **A laughter** N. 36–7 N.
41 **miss't** avoid the conventional phraseology (cf. l. 26 above).
43 **temperance** temperature, climate. 44 **Temperance** common
Puritan name for a woman. 45 **subtle** here, 'crafty,' 'sly.'

Antonio. Or as 'twere perfum'd by a fen.   49

Gonzalo. Here is everything advantageous to life.

Antonio. True, save means to live.

Sebastian. Of that there's none, or little.

Gonzalo. How lush and lusty the grass looks! How green!

Antonio. The ground indeed is tawny.   55

Sebastian. With an eye of green in't.

Antonio. He misses not much.

Sebastian. No—he doth but mistake the truth totally.   59

Gonzalo. But the rarity of it is—which is indeed almost beyond credit—

Sebastian. As many vouch'd rarities are—

Gonzalo. That our garments being—as they were—drench'd in the sea, hold, notwithstanding, their freshness and glosses, being rather new-dy'd than stain'd with salt water.   66

Antonio. If but one of his pockets could speak, would it not say he lies?

Sebastian. Ay, or very falsely pocket up his report.

Gonzalo. Methinks our garments are now as fresh as when we put them on first in Afric, at the marriage of the king's fair daughter Claribel to the King of Tunis.   73

Sebastian. 'Twas a sweet marriage, and we prosper well in our return.

Adrian. Tunis was never grac'd before with such a paragon to their queen.

Gonzalo. Not since widow Dido's time.

Antonio. Widow? A pox o' that! How came that widow in? Widow Dido!   80

53 lusty strong. 55 tawny brown. 57 misses not much doesn't miss by much. 65 glosses N. 77 to for 80 Widow Dido N.

Sebastian. What if he had said 'widower Aeneas' too? Good lord, how you take it!

Adrian. 'Widow Dido' said you? You make me study of that. She was of Carthage, not of Tunis.

Gonzalo. This Tunis, sir, was Carthage.   85

Adrian. Carthage?

Gonzalo. I assure you, Carthage.

Antonio. His word is more than the miraculous harp.   89

Sebastian. He hath rais'd the wall, and houses too.

Antonio. What impossible matter will he make easy next?

Sebastian. I think he will carry this island home in his pocket and give it his son for an apple.   94

Antonio. And sowing the kernels of it in the sea, bring forth more islands.

Gonzalo. [*Having pondered.*] Ay.

Antonio. Why, in good time.

Gonzalo. Sir, we were talking that our garments seem now as fresh as when we were at Tunis at the marriage of your daughter, who is now queen.   101

Antonio. And the rarest that ere came there.

Sebastian. Bate, I beseech you, widow Dido.

Antonio. Oh, widow Dido? Ay, widow Dido!   104

Gonzalo. Is not, sir, my doublet as fresh as the first day I wore it? I mean, in a sort.

Antonio. That sort was well fish'd for.

Gonzalo. When I wore it at your daughter's marriage—   109

Alonso. You cram these words into mine ears against

88–89 **miraculous harp** of Zeus' son, who with his playing raised the walls of Thebes. 90 **houses too** i.e. by claiming Carthage still exists as Tunis. 97 **Ay** in reaffirmation that Tunis was Carthage (Kittredge); F spells it *I*. 103 **Bate** except for. 106 **in a sort** after a fashion. 107 **fish'd for** N.

The stomach of my sense. Would I had never
Married my daughter there, for coming thence
My son is lost and—in my rate—she too,
Who is so far from Italy remov'd
I ne're again shall see her. O thou mine heir   115
Of Naples and of Milan, what strange fish
Hath made his meal on thee?

  Francisco.   Sir, he may live.
I saw him beat the surges under him
And ride upon their backs; he trod the water,
Whose enmity he flung aside, and breasted   120
The surge most swolne that met him. His bold head
'Bove the contentious waves he kept, and oared
Himself with his good arms in lusty stroke
To th' shore, that ore his wave-worn basis bowed
As stooping to relieve him. I not doubt   125
He came alive to land.

  Alonso.   No, no, he's gone.
  Sebastian. Sir, you may thank yourself for this
    great loss
That would not bless our Europe with your daughter,
But rather loose her to an African,
Where she at least is banish'd from your eye,   130
Who hath cause to wet the grief on't.

  Alonso.   Prithee peace.
  Sebastian. You were kneel'd to and importun'd
    otherwise
By all of us, and the fair soul herself
Weigh'd, between loathness and obedience, at   134

111 **stomach** inclination. **sense** feelings. 113 **rate** estimation.
124 **basis** trunk. 125 **As** as if. 129 **loose** mate. 131 **Who . . . on't**
which has reason to shed tears upon the grief revealed in it.
Who hath probably pronounced 'Who'th.' 134 **Weigh'd** forced to
choose.

Which end o' th' beam should bow. We have lost your
    son,
I fear, for ever: Milan and Naples have
Mo widows in them of this business' making
Than we bring men to comfort them.
The fault's your own.

    Alonso.   So is the dear'st o' th' loss.

    Gonzalo. My Lord Sebastian,   140
The truth you speak doth lack some gentleness,
And time to speak it in: you rub the sore
When you should bring the plaster.

    Sebastian.   Very well.

    Antonio. And most chirurgeonly.

    Gonzalo. It is foul weather in us all, good sir, 145
When you are cloudy.

    Sebastian.   *Fowl* weather?

    Antonio.   Very foul.

    Gonzalo. Had I plantation of this isle, my lord—

    Antonio. He'd sow't with nettle seed.

    Sebastian.   Or docks, or
    mallows.   148

    Gonzalo. And were the king on't, what would I do?

    Sebastian. 'Scape being drunk, for want of wine.

    Gonzalo. I' th' commonwealth I would by contraries
Execute all things; for no kind of traffic
Would I admit; no name of magistrate;

---

137 **Mo** more. 139 **dear'st** 'most dearly loved' and 'of highest
worth' ('what touches one most nearly'—Arden ed.). 142 **time**
fitting time. 143 **Very well** very well spoken (sarcasm). 144 **chi-
rurgeonly** like a surgeon. 146 **Fowl** N. **foul** i.e. 'a very foul pun'—
to be balanced against 'Very well' of l. 143, above. 147 **plantation**
colonization, purposely misconstrued by Antonio in the next
line. 148 **docks, or mallows** weeds. 149 **on't** of it. 151–73 N.

Letters should not be known; riches, poverty,
And use of service, none; contract, succession,   155
Bourn, bound of land, tilth, vineyard, none;
No use of metal, corn, or wine, or oil;
No occupation—all men idle, all;
And women too, but innocent and pure;
No sovereignty.   160

  Sebastian. Yet he would be king on't.

  Antonio. The latter end of his commonwealth forgets the beginning.

  Gonzalo. All things in common nature should produce,
Without sweat or endeavor; treason, felony,   165
Sword, pike, knife, gun, or need of any engine
Would I not have; but Nature should bring forth
Of it own kind all foison, all abundance,
To feed my innocent people.

  Sebastian. No marrying 'mong his subjects?   170

  Antonio. None, man; all idle: whores and knaves.

  Gonzalo. I would with such perfection govern, sir,
T'excel the Golden Age.

  Sebastian.   'Save his Majesty!

  Antonio. Long live Gonzalo!

  Gonzalo.   And—do you mark me,
    sir?

  Alonso. Prithee no more; thou dost talk nothing
to me.   175

  Gonzalo. I do well believe your Highness, and did it

---

155 **use of service** custom of employing servants. **contract** stressed
— ⌣. **succession** inheritance. 156 **Bourn** boundary. **tilth** tilled
land. 166 **engine** machine used in warfare. 168 **it** its. **foison** plentiful harvest. 173 **T'excel** as to excel. **'Save** God save N. 175
nothing nonsense.

to minister occasion to these gentlemen, who are of
such sensible and nimble lungs that they always use
to laugh at nothing.

Antonio. 'Twas you we laugh'd at.   180

Gonzalo. Who in this kind of merry fooling am nothing to you; so you may continue and laugh at nothing
still.

Antonio. What a blow was there given!

Sebastian. And it had not falne flat-long.   185

Gonzalo. You are gentlemen of brave metal; you
would lift the moon out of her sphere, if she would
continue in it five weeks without changing.

Enter Ariel playing solemn music.

Sebastian. We would so, and then go a-batfowling.

Antonio. Nay, good my lord, be not angry.   190

Gonzalo. No, I warrant you; I will not adventure
my discretion so weakly. Will you laugh me asleep?
for I am very heavy.

Antonio. Go sleep, and hear us.   194

[*All sleep but Alonso, Sebastian, and Antonio.*]

Alonso. What, all so soon asleep? I wish mine eyes
Would, with themselves, shut up my thoughts. I find
They are inclin'd to do so.

Sebastian.   Please you, sir,
Do not omit the heavy offer of it.

---

178 **sensible** sensitive. **nimble** active. 180 **you** i.e. 'nothing.'
182 **to you** compared with you. 185 **And** if. **falne** fallen. **flat-long**
with the flat of the sword. 186 **metal** modern 'mettle.' 187 **sphere**
N. 187–8 **if . . . changing** if it would wait an impossible time
(longer than the lunar month). 189 **go a-batfowling** N. 191–2
adventure my discretion hazard my reputation. 194 **hear us**
i.e. 'hear us laugh.' 198 **omit** neglect. **offer** invitation.

It seldom visits sorrow; when it doth
It is a comforter.

Antonio.   We two, my lord,   200
Will guard your person while you take your rest,
And watch your safety.

Alonso.   Thank you. Wondrous
  heavy . . .   [*Alonso sleeps. Exit Ariel.*]

Sebastian. What a strange drowsiness possesses
  them!

Antonio. It is the quality o' th' climate.

Sebastian.   Why
Doth it not then our eyelids sink? I find not   205
Myself dispos'd to sleep.

Antonio.   Nor I: my spirits are nimble.
They fell together all as by consent;
They dropp'd as by a thunderstroke. What might,
Worthy Sebastian? O what might—? No more!
And yet, methinks I see it in thy face,   210
What thou shouldst be; th' occasion speaks thee, and
My strong imagination sees a crown
Dropping upon thy head.

Sebastian.   What? Art thou waking?

Antonio. Do you not hear me speak?

Sebastian.   I do, and surely
It is a sleepy language, and thou speak'st   215
Out of thy sleep! What is it thou didst say?
This is a strange repose, to be asleep
With eyes wide open—standing, speaking, moving,
And yet so fast asleep.

Antonio.   Noble Sebastian,   219
Thou let'st thy fortune sleep—die rather; wink'st

199–202 N. 205 sink cause to close. 207 consent agreement.
211 speaks thee 'proclaims thee king,' or 'speaks to thee.' 220
wink'st i.e. 'art oblivious to thy opportunity.'

Whiles thou art waking.

Sebastian.   Thou dost snore distinctly:
There's meaning in thy snores.

Antonio. I am more serious than my custom—you
Must be so too, if heed me; which to do
Trebles thee ore.

Sebastian.   Well, I am standing water.   225

Antonio. I'll teach you how to flow.

Sebastian.   Do so: to ebb
Hereditary sloth instructs me.

Antonio.   O,
If you but knew how you the purpose cherish
Whiles thus you mock it, how in stripping it
You more invest it! ebbing men indeed—   230
Most often—do so near the bottom run
By their own fear or sloth.

Sebastian.   Prithee say on;
The setting of thine eye and cheek proclaim
A matter from thee, and a birth, indeed,
Which throes thee much to yield.

Antonio.   Thus, sir: 235
Although this lord of weak remembrance, this
Who shall be of as little memory
When he is earth'd, hath here almost persuaded—
For he's a spirit of persuasion, only   239

221 **distinctly** explained by the next line. 225 **Trebles thee ore**
triples thy value. **standing water** unmoving, between ebb and
flood. 226 **flow** rise (like the tide). 229–30 **stripping . . . invest**
a clothing metaphor: to invest is to clothe with robes of office.
233 **setting** rigid expression. 235 **throes thee** causes thee agony
(as of childbirth). 236 **this lord** probably Gonzalo, who supported
Francisco's account and aroused Antonio's scorn. 238 **earth'd**
buried. 239–40 **For . . . persuade** for he's persuasion personified,
whose only profession is to persuade.

36

Professes to persuade—the king his son's alive,
'Tis as impossible that he's undrown'd
As he that sleeps here swims.

  Sebastian.   **I have no hope**
That he's undrown'd.

  Antonio.   O, out of that 'no hope'
What great hope have you! No hope that way is
Another way so high a hope that even   245
Ambition cannot pierce a wink beyond
But doubt discovery there. Will you grant with me
That Ferdinand is drown'd?

  Sebastian.   He's gone.

  Antonio.   Then tell me,
Who's the next heir of Naples?

  Sebastian.   Claribel.   249

  Antonio. She that is Queen of Tunis ; she that dwells
Ten leagues beyond man's life ; she that from Naples
Can have no note, unless the sun were post—
The man i' th' moon's too slow—till new-born chins
Be rough and razorable ; she that from whom   254
We all were sea-swallow'd, though some cast again—
And by that destiny—to perform an act
Whereof what's past is prologue, what to come
In yours and my discharge.

  Sebastian.   What stuff is this?
How say you?   259
'Tis true my brother's daughter's Queen of Tunis ;
So is she heir of Naples ; 'twixt which regions
There is some space.

242 hope N. 247 But doubt discovery without putting out the
light of discovery: to 'dout' (do out) was to 'extinguish.' there a
state greater than the kingship of Naples. 252 note information.
post messenger. 255 cast play on the meanings 'disgorged' and
'assigned to parts in a play' ; cf. following lines. 257–8 what . . .
discharge N.

Antonio.   A space whose ev'ry cubit
Seems to cry out, 'How shall that Claribel
Measure us back to Naples? Keep in Tunis
And let Sebastian wake!' Say this were death   265
That now hath seiz'd them, why they were no worse
Than now they are; there be that can rule Naples
As well as he that sleeps, lords that can prate
As amply and unnecessarily
As this Gonzalo—I myself could make   270
A chough of as deep chat—O that you bore
The mind that I do! What a sleep were this
For your advancement! Do you understand me?
Sebastian. Methinks I do.
Antonio.   And how does your content
Tender your own good fortune?
Sebastian.   I remember   275
You did supplant your brother Prospero.
Antonio.   True.
And look how well my garments sit upon me,
Much feater than before. My brother's servants
Were then my fellows; now they are my men.
Sebastian. But for your conscience—   280
Antonio. Ay, sir, where lies that? If 'twere a kibe
'Twould put me to my slipper; but I feel not
This deity in my bosom; twenty consciences
That stand 'twixt me and Milan, candied be they
And melt, ere they molest! Here lies your brother,
No better than the earth he lies upon,   286
If he were that which now he's like—that's dead—
Whom I with this obedient steel—three inches of it—

264 **Measure** journey across. 267 **there be that** there be those who.
270–1 I . . . **chat** I could make of myself a jackdaw capable of
Gonzalo's prattle. 274 **content** liking. 275 **Tender** regard. 278
feater more fitly. 281 **kibe** chilblain, or sore on heel. 284 **candied**
congealed. 285 **molest** worry me.

Can lay to bed forever; whiles you, doing thus,
To the perpetual wink for aye might put   290
This ancient morsel, this Sir Prudence, who
Should not upbraid our course. For all the rest,
They'll take suggestion as a cat laps milk;
They'll tell the clock to any business that
We say befits the hour.
    Sebastian.   Thy case, dear friend,   295
Shall be my precedent: as thou got'st Milan
I'll come by Naples. Draw thy sword; one stroke
Shall free thee from the tribute which thou payest,
And I the king shall love thee.
  Antonio.   Draw together;
And when I rear my hand do you the like,   300
To fall it on Gonzalo.
  Sebastian.   O, but one word.

                              [They converse apart.]

           Enter Ariel with music and song.

Ariel. My master through his art foresees the danger
That you, his friend, are in and sends me forth—
For else his project dies—to keep them living.
                        Sings in Gonzalo's ear.

           [Song]

     While you here do snoring lie,   305
     Open-ey'd Conspiracy
       His time doth take.
     If of life you keep a care,
     Shake off slumber and beware.
       Awake, awake!   310

Antonio. Then let us both be sudden.

294 tell . . . to say the time is ripe for.

Gonzalo. [*Awakening.*]   Now, good
    angels,
Preserve the king!   [*Shakes Alonso.*]
    Alonso. Why, how now, ho! awake? Why are you
    drawn?
Wherefore this ghastly looking?
    Gonzalo.   What's the matter?
    Sebastian. Whiles we stood here securing your re-
    pose—   315
Even now—we heard a hollow burst of bellowing
Like bulls, or rather lions—did't not wake you?
It struck mine ear most terribly.
    Alonso.   I heard nothing.
    Antonio. O, 'twas a din to fright a monster's ear,
To make an earthquake! Sure it was the roar   320
Of a whole herd of lions.
    Alonso.   Heard you this, Gonzalo?
    Gonzalo. Upon mine honor, sir, I heard a hum-
    ming—
And that a strange one too—which did awake me.
I shak'd you, sir, and cried; as mine eyes open'd
I saw their weapons drawn—there was a noise,   325
That's verily! 'Tis best we stand upon our guard,
Or that we quit this place. Let's draw our weapons.
    Alonso. Lead off this ground and let's make further
    search
For my poor son.
    Gonzalo.   Heavens keep him from these
    beasts,
For he is sure i' th' island.
    Alonso.   Lead away.   330
    Ariel. Prospero, my lord, shall know what I have
    done.

318 struck F *strook.*

40

So, king, go safely on to seek thy son.   *Exeunt.*

SCENE 2

*Enter Caliban with a burthen of wood. A noise of
thunder heard.*

Caliban. All the infections that the sun sucks up
From bogs, fens, flats on Prosper fall, and make him
By inchmeal a disease! His spirits hear me,
And yet I needs must curse. But they'll nor pinch,
Fright me with urchin-shows, pitch me i' th' mire,   5
Nor lead me like a firebrand in the dark
Out of my way, unless he bid 'em; but
For every trifle are they set upon me,
Sometime like apes that mow and chatter at me
And after bite me, then like hedgehogs which   10
Lie tumbling in my barefoot way and mount
Their pricks at my footfall; sometime am I
All wound with adders, who with cloven tongues
Do hiss me into madness.

Enter Trinculo.

                    Lo, now, lo!
Here comes a spirit of his, and to torment me   15
For bringing wood in slowly! I'll fall flat.
Perchance he will not mind me.
    Trinculo. Here's neither bush nor shrub to bear off
any weather at all, and another storm brewing. I

---

3 **By inchmeal** little by little (cf. modern 'piecemeal'). 6 **firebrand**
ignis fatuus (will-o'-the-wisp). 9 **mow** grimace. 18 **bear** ward.

hear it sing i' th' wind. Yond same black cloud, yond huge one, looks like a foul bombard that would shed his liquor. If it should thunder, as it did before, I know not where to hide my head. Yond same cloud cannot choose but fall by pailfuls. [*Sees Caliban.*] What have we here, a man? or a fish? dead or alive? A fish. He smells like a fish—a very ancient and fish-like smell—a kind of, not of the newest, poor-john—a strange fish! Were I in England now—as once I was—and had but this fish painted, not a holiday fool there but would give a piece of silver; there would this monster make a man: any strange beast there makes a man! When they will not give a doit to relieve a lame beggar, they will lay out ten to see a dead Indian. Legg'd like a man, and his fins like arms! Warm, o' my troth! I do now let loose my opinion, hold it no longer: this is no fish but an islander, that hath lately suffered by a thunderbolt. [*Thunder.*] Alas, the storm is come again! My best way is to creep under his gaberdine: there is no other shelter hereabout. Misery acquaints a man with strange bed-fellows! I will here shroud till the dregs of the storm be past.   [*Creeps under Caliban's garment.*]

Enter Stephano singing.

Stephano. I shall no more to sea, to sea;
Here shall I die ashore.

44

21 **bombard** leather wine jug. 27 **poor-john** salt hake (a kind of fish). 29 **painted** i.e. on a board to advertise the exhibition (cf. *Macbeth*, V.7.54–5); Malone cites many references to this practice. 31 **make a man** make a man's fortune (with a pun, explained in the following clause). 32 **doit** almost worthless Dutch coin. 34 **dead Indian** such as were displayed in England, in the Elizabethan equivalent of a side show. 39 **gaberdine** cloak. 41 **shroud** take shelter.

This is a very scurvy tune to sing at a man's funeral!
Well, here's my comfort.   *Drinks [and then] sings.*

[Song]

The master, the swabber, the boatswain, and I,
The gunner and his mate
Lov'd Moll, Meg, and Marian, and Margery,
But none of us car'd for Kate.   50
For she had a tongue with a tang,
Would cry to a sailor, go hang!
She lov'd not the savor of tar nor of pitch,
Yet a tailor might scratch her wherere she did itch.
Then to sea, boys, and let her go hang!   55

This is a scurvy tune, too: but here's my comfort.
                                         Drinks.

Caliban. Do not torment me! O!

Stephano. What's the matter? Have we divels here?
Do you put tricks upon's with salvages and men of
Inde? ha? I have not 'scap'd drowning to be afeard
now of your four legs; for it hath bin said, 'as proper
a man as ever went on four legs cannot make him
give ground,' and it shall be said so again, while
Stephano breathes at' nostrils.

Caliban. The spirit torments me! O!   65

Stephano. This is some monster of the isle with four
legs, who hath got—as I take it—an ague. Where
the divel should he learn our language? I will give
him some relief if it be but for that! If I can recover
him and keep him tame, and get to Naples with him,
he's a present for any emperor that ever trod on
neat's leather.

47 **swabber** one who kept the ship clean. 59 **salvages** savages.
69 **recover** restore. 72 **neat's leather** leather from cattle of the ox
kind.

                            43

Caliban. Do not torment me, prithee! I'll bring my wood home faster. 74

Stephano. He's in his fit now, and does not talk after the wisest. He shall taste of my bottle! If he have never drunk wine afore, it will go near to remove his fit. If I can recover him and keep him tame, I will not take too much for him; he shall pay for him that hath him, and that soundly. 80

Caliban. Thou dost me yet but little hurt. Thou wilt anon; I know it by thy trembling. Now Prosper works upon thee. 83

Stephano. Come on your ways—open your mouth —here is that which will give language to you, cat. Open your mouth! This will shake your shaking, I can tell you, and that soundly. You cannot tell who's your friend. Open your chaps again. 88

Trinculo. I should know that voice! It should be— but he is drown'd, and these are divels. O defend me!

Stephano. Four legs and two voices—a most delicate monster! His forward voice now is to speak well of his friend; his backward voice is to utter foul speeches and to detract. If all the wine in my bottle will recover him, I will help his ague. Come! Amen! I will pour some in thy other mouth. 96

Trinculo. Stephano!

Stephano. Doth thy other mouth call me? Mercy, mercy! This is a divel and no monster! I will leave him: I have no long spoon. 100

Trinculo. Stephano! If thou beest Stephano, touch

79 I . . . **him** no price will be too high for him. 82 **thy trembling** i.e. Trinculo's. 85 **language** . . . **cat** in reference to an old proverb, 'Liquor will make a cat speak.' 100 **long spoon** in reference to the proverb, 'He that would eat with the devil needs a long spoon.'

me and speak to me, for I am Trinculo—be not
afeard—thy good friend Trinculo.   103

Stephano. If thou beest Trinculo, come forth! I'll
pull thee by the lesser legs. If any be Trinculo's legs,
these are they . . . Thou art very Trinculo indeed!
How cam'st thou to be the siege of this mooncalf?
Can he vent Trinculos?   108

Trinculo. I took him to be kill'd with a thunderstroke. But art thou not drown'd, Stephano? I hope
now thou art not drown'd! Is the storm over-blown?
I hid me under the dead mooncalf's gaberdine, for
fear of the storm. And art thou living, Stephano?
O Stephano, two Neapolitans 'scap'd?   114

Stephano. Prithee do not turn me about—my stomach is not constant.

Caliban. These be fine things and if they be not
sprites! That's a brave god, and bears celestial liquor. I will kneel to him.   119

Stephano. How didst thou 'scape? How cam'st thou
hither? Swear by this bottle how thou cam'st hither!
I escap'd upon a butt of sack which the sailors heaved
oreboard, by this bottle! which I made of the bark
of a tree with mine own hands since I was cast ashore.

Caliban. I'll swear upon that bottle to be thy true
subject, for the liquor is not earthly.   126

Stephano. Here! Swear then how thou escap'dst.

Trinculo. Swum ashore, man, like a duck! I can swim
like a duck, I'll be sworn.   129

Stephano. Here, kiss the book. [*Trinculo drinks.*]

---

107 **siege** excrement. **mooncalf** a *mooncalf* was a shapeless abor-
tion, thought to be caused by the action of the moon. 117 **and
if** if. 130 **kiss the book** joking reference to the custom of kissing
the Bible after swearing on it; see l. 125 above.

Though thou canst swim like a duck, thou art made like a goose.

Trinculo. O Stephano, hast any more of this?

Stephano. The whole butt, man! My cellar is in a rock by th' seaside, where my wine is hid. How now, mooncalf? How does thine ague?   136

Caliban. Hast thou not dropp'd from heaven?

Stephano. Out o' th' moon, I do assure thee. I was the man i' th' moon, when time was.   139

Caliban. I have seen thee in her—and I do adore thee! My mistress show'd me thee, and thy dog, and thy bush.

Stephano. Come, swear to that! Kiss the book! I will furnish it anon with new contents! Swear.   144

[*Caliban drinks.*]

Trinculo. By this good light, this is a very shallow monster! I afeard of him? a very weak monster! The man i' th' moon? A most poor credulous monster! Well drawn, monster, in good sooth.

Caliban. I'll show thee every fertile inch o' th' island —and I will kiss thy foot! I prithee, be my god.   150

Trinculo. By this light, a most perfidious and drunken monster; when's god's asleep he'll rob his bottle.

Caliban. I'll kiss thy foot. I'll swear myself thy subject.   155

Stephano. Come on, then—down and swear.

Trinculo. I shall laugh myself to death at this puppy-headed monster! A most scurvy monster! I could find in my heart to beat him—

139 **when time was** once upon a time. 141–2 **thy dog . . . bush** in reference to an old tale that the man in the moon was banished there with his dog for gathering brush on Sunday. 148 **drawn** drunk.

Stephano. Come, kiss.   160

Trinculo. But that the poor monster's in drink. An abominable monster!

Caliban. I'll show thee the best springs; I'll pluck
    thee berries;
I'll fish for thee, and get thee wood enough.
A plague upon the tyrant that I serve!   165
I'll bear him no more sticks, but follow thee,
Thou wondrous man.

Trinculo. A most ridiculous monster, to make a wonder of a poor drunkard.

Caliban. I prithee let me bring thee where crabs
    grow;   170
And I with my long nails will dig thee pignuts,
Show thee a jay's nest, and instruct thee how
To snare the nimble marmoset; I'll bring thee
To clust'ring filberts, and sometimes I'll get thee 174
Young scamels from the rock. Wilt thou go with me?

Stephano. I prithee now, lead the way without any more talking. Trinculo, the king and all our company else being drown'd, we will inherit here. Here, bear my bottle! Fellow Trinculo, we'll fill him by and by again.
    Caliban sings drunkenly.

Caliban. Farewell, master; farewell, farewell!   180

Trinculo. A howling monster! a drunken monster!

Caliban. [*Singing.*] No more dams I'll make for fish,
    Nor fetch in firing
    At requiring,   184
    Nor scrape trenchering, nor wash dish.

170 crabs crabapples. **175 scamels** probably the bird called the sea mell (mew). **179 by and by** right away. **185 trenchering** trenchers.

> *'Ban, 'Ban, Ca-Caliban*
> *Has a new master—get a new man.*

Freedom, high-day! high-day, freedom! freedom, high-day, freedom! 189

Stephano. O brave monster! lead the way. *Exeunt.*

188 **high-day** heyday.

48

Act III

SCENE 1

Enter Ferdinand, bearing a log.

Ferdinand. There be some sports are painful, and
    their labor
Delight in them sets off; some kinds of baseness
Are nobly undergone, and most poor matters
Point to rich ends. This my mean task
Would be as heavy to me as odious, but   5
The mistress which I serve quickens what's dead
And makes my labors pleasures. O she is
Ten times more gentle than her father's crabbed,
And he's compos'd of harshness. I must remove
Some thousands of these logs and pile them up,   10
Upon a sore injunction. My sweet mistress
Weeps when she sees me work, and says such baseness
Had never like executor. I forget;
But these sweet thoughts do even refresh my labors,
Most busy lest, when I do it.

*Enter Miranda and Prospero [behind her and
    unseen].*

Miranda.   Alas, now pray you
Work not so hard! I would the lightning had   16
Burnt up those logs that you are enjoin'd to pile:

1 **be** are. **are** which are. **painful** laborious. 2 **Delight . . . off**
the pleasure they arouse compensates for their labor. **sets** F *set.*
11 **Upon . . . injunction** on pain of severe punishment. 13 **I
forget** i.e. my task. 15 **lest** least. **Most . . . it** N.

49

Pray set it down and rest you; when this burns
'Twill weep for having wearied you. My father
Is hard at study; pray now rest yourself: 20
He's safe for these three hours.

   Ferdinand.   O most dear mistress,
The sun will set before I shall discharge
What I must strive to do.

   Miranda.   If you'll sit down
I'll bear your logs the while—pray give me that;
I'll carry it to the pile.

   Ferdinand.   No, precious creature,   25
I had rather crack my sinews, break my back,
Than you should such dishonor undergo
While I sit lazy by.

   Miranda.   It would become me
As well as it does you, and I should do it
With much more ease, for my good will is to it   30
And yours it is against.

   Prospero.   Poor worm, thou art in-
     fected;
This visitation shows it.

   Miranda.   You look wearily.

   Ferdinand. No, noble mistress, 'tis fresh morning
     with me
When you are by at night. I do beseech you,
Chiefly that I might set it in my prayers,   35
What is your name?

   Miranda.   Miranda. O my father,
I have broke your hest to say so.

   Ferdinand.   Admir'd Miranda,
Indeed the top of admiration, worth

19 **'Twill weep** the sap (or pitch) will look like tears. 32 **visitation**
N. 37 **hest** command. **Admir'd Miranda** a play on Miranda's
name.

What's dearest to the world: full many a lady
I have ey'd with best regard, and many a time   40
Th' harmony of their tongues hath into bondage
Brought my too diligent ear; for several virtues
Have I lik'd several women, never any
With so full soul, but some defect in her
Did quarrel with the noblest grace she ow'd   45
And put it to the foil. But you, O you,
So perfect and so peerless, are created
Of every creature's best.
  Miranda.   I do not know
One of my sex, no woman's face remember
Save from my glass mine own, nor have I seen   50
More that I may call men than you, good friend,
And my dear father: how features are abroad
I am skilless of; but by my modesty—
The jewel in my dower—I would not wish
Any companion in the world but you;   55
Nor can imagination form a shape
Besides yourself to like of. But I prattle
Something too wildly and my father's precepts
I therein do forget.
  Ferdinand.   I am, in my condition,
A prince, Miranda—I do think a king—   60
I would not so—and would no more endure
This wooden slavery than to suffer
The flesh-fly blow my mouth. Hear my soul speak:
The very instant that I saw you did
My heart fly to your service, there resides   65

---

45 ow'd owned. 46 put . . . foil 'challenged it to a fencing match,'
with a play on *foil* in the sense of 'defeat' (OED). 47 peerless F
peetlesse. 53 skilless ignorant. 59 condition rank. 59–63 N. 63
flesh-fly a fly which lays its eggs in dead flesh. blow sully.

To make me slave to it and for your sake
Am I this patient log-man.
    Miranda.   **Do** you love me?
    Ferdinand. **O** heaven, **O** earth, bear witness to this
        sound,
And crown what I profess with kind event
If I speak true; if hollowly, invert   70
What best is boded me to mischief: I,
Beyond all limit of what else i' th' world
Do love, prize, honor you.
    Miranda.   **I** am a fool
To weep at what I am glad of.
    Prospero.   **Fair** encounter
Of two most rare affections! Heavens rain grace   75
On that which breeds between 'em.
    Ferdinand.   **Wherefore** weep
        you?
    Miranda. At mine unworthiness, that dare not offer
What I desire to give and much less take
What I shall die to want. But this is trifling
And all the more it seeks to hide itself   80
The bigger bulk it shows. Hence, bashful cunning,
And prompt me, plain and holy innocence.
I am your wife if you will marry me;
If not I'll die your maid. To be your fellow
You may deny me, but I'll be your servant   85
Whether you will or no.
    Ferdinand.   **My** mistress, dearest!
And I thus humble ever.
    Miranda.   **My** husband, then?

69 event outcome. **70 hollowly** falsely. **70–1 invert . . . mischief**
turn into bad fortune all the good that is to befall me. **72 what**
anything. **84 maid** play on 'maidservant' and 'unmarried woman';
cf. following line. **fellow** mate, equal.

Ferdinand. Ay, with a heart as willing
As bondage ere of freedom! Here's my hand.
    Miranda. And mine, with my heart in't; and now
      farewell   90
Till half an hour hence.
    Ferdinand.   A thousand thousand!
                                 Exeunt.

    Prospero. So glad of this as they I cannot be
Who are surpris'd with all, but my rejoicing
At nothing can be more! I'll to my book,
For yet ere supper time must I perform   95
Much business appertaining.   *Exit.*

SCENE 2

Enter Caliban, Stephano, and Trinculo.

    Stephano. Tell not me—when the butt is out we will
drink water, not a drop before; therefore bear up
and board 'em. Servant monster, drink to me.   3
    Trinculo. Servant monster? The folly of this island!
They say there's but five upon this isle; we are three
of them. If th' other two be brain'd like us, the state
totters.
    Stephano. Drink, servant monster, when I bid thee.
Thy eyes are almost set in thy head.   9
    Trinculo. Where should they be set else? He were a
brave monster indeed if they were set in his tail.

89 **bondage . . . freedom** one in bondage ever welcomed freedom. 93 **with all** i.e. all that has happened (or perhaps *withal*,
'thereby,' is meant). 2–3 **bear . . . 'em** obvious nautical phraseology. 9 **set** fixed in a stare. 10 **were** would be. 11 **brave** admirable.

Stephano. My man-monster hath drown'd his tongue in sack. For my part, the sea cannot drown me. I swam ere I could recover the shore, five and thirty leagues off and on. By this light thou shalt be my lieutenant, monster, or my standard.   16

Trinculo. Your lieutenant, if you list—he's no standard.

Stephano. We'll not run, Monsieur Monster.

Trinculo. Nor go neither; but you'll lie like dogs, and yet say nothing, neither.   21

Stephano. Mooncalf, speak once in thy life, if thou beest a good mooncalf.

Caliban. How does thy honor? Let me lick thy shoe. I'll not serve *him*—he is not valiant.   25

Trinculo. Thou liest, most ignorant monster! I am in case to justle a constable! Why, thou debosh'd fish, thou, was there ever man a coward that hath drunk so much sack as I today? Wilt thou tell a monstrous lie, being but half a fish and half a monster?

Caliban. Lo, how he mocks me! Wilt thou let him, my lord?

Trinculo. 'Lord,' quoth he? That a monster should be such a natural!   34

Caliban. Lo, lo again! Bite him to death, I prithee!

Stephano. Trinculo, keep a good tongue in your head! If you prove a mutineer—the next tree! The poor monster's my subject and he shall not suffer indignity.   39

17 list meaning both 'desire' and 'careen.' 18 standard meaning both 'ensign' (standard bearer) and 'support' (for Stephano, who, like Caliban, is tipsy). 19 run *double-entendre* ('run from an enemy' and 'excrete'). 20 lie double-entendre ('prevaricate' and 'excrete'). 27 case condition. debosh'd debauched. 34 natural idiot.

Caliban. I thank my noble lord. Wilt thou be pleas'd
to hearken once again to the suit I made to thee?

Stephano. Marry will I. Kneel and repeat it. I will
stand and so shall Trinculo.

Enter Ariel, invisible.

Caliban. As I told thee before, I am subject to a
tyrant, a sorcerer, that by his cunning hath cheated
me of the island.   46

Ariel. Thou liest.

Caliban. [*To Trinculo.*] *Thou* liest, thou jesting
monkey, thou! I would my valiant master would destroy thee. I do not lie.   50

Stephano. Trinculo, if you trouble him any more
in's tale, by this hand I will supplant some of your
teeth.

Trinculo. Why, I said nothing.

Stephano. Mum, then, and no more! Proceed.   55

Caliban. I say by sorcery he got this isle
From me, he got it. If thy greatness will,
Revenge it on him—for I know thou dar'st
But this thing dare not.

Stephano. That's most certain.   60

Caliban. Thou shalt be lord of it, and I'll serve thee.

Stephano. How now shall this be compass'd? Canst
thou bring me to the party?

Caliban. Yea, yea, my lord, I'll yield him thee asleep
Where thou may'st knock a nail into his head.   65

Ariel. Thou liest. Thou canst not.

Caliban. What a pied ninny's this? Thou scurvy
          patch!
I do beseech thy greatness, give him blows

59 **thing** Trinculo. 67 **pied ninny** fool in motley. 68 **patch** dolt.

And take his bottle from him! When that's gone   69
He shall drink nought but brine, for I'll not show him
Where the quick freshes are.

   Stephano. Trinculo, run into no further danger!
Interrupt the monster one word further and by this
hand I'll turn my mercy out o' doors and make a
stockfish of thee.   75

   Trinculo. Why what did I? I did nothing! I'll go
farther off.

   Stephano. Didst thou not say he lied?

   Ariel. Thou liest.   79

   Stephano. Do I so? Take thou that! [*Hits Trinculo.*] As you like this, give me the lie another time.

   Trinculo. I did not give the lie! Out o' your wits,
and hearing too? A pox o' your bottle. This can sack
and drinking do! A murrain on your monster and the
divel take your fingers!   85

   Caliban. Ha ha ha!

   Stephano. Now forward with your tale! [*To Trinculo.*] Prithee stand further off.

   Caliban. Beat him enough! After a little time I'll
beat him too.   90

   Stephano. Stand farther! [*To Caliban.*] Come, proceed.

   Caliban. Why, as I told thee, 'tis a custom with him
I' th' afternoon to sleep; there thou mayst brain him,
Having first seiz'd his books, or with a log   95
Batter his skull, or paunch him with a stake,
Or cut his wezand with thy knife. Remember
First to possess his books, for without them
He's but a sot, as I am, nor hath not

71 **quick freshes** springs. 75 **stockfish** dried cod which had to be
beaten soft before it could be cooked. 84 **murrain** cattle disease.
97 **wezand** windpipe. 99 **sot** fool.

   56

One spirit to command: they all do hate him   100
As rootedly as I. Burn but his books.
He has brave utensils—for so he calls them—
Which when he has a house he'll deck withal.
And that most deeply to consider is
The beauty of his daughter: he himself   105
Calls her a nonpareil. I never saw a woman
But only Sycorax my dam and she;
But she as far surpasseth Sycorax
As great'st does least.
   Stephano.   Is it so brave a lass?
   Caliban. Ay, lord, she will become thy bed, I war-
      rant,   110
And bring thee forth brave brood.
   Stephano. Monster, I will kill this man! His daugh-
ter and I will be king and queen, save our Graces!
and Trinculo and thyself shall be viceroys! Dost thou
like the plot, Trinculo?   115
   Trinculo. Excellent.
   Stephano. Give me thy hand; I am sorry I beat thee!
But while thou liv'st keep a good tongue in thy head.
   Caliban. Within this half hour will he be asleep.
Wilt thou destroy him then?
   Stephano.   Ay, on my honor.   120
   Ariel. This will I tell my master.
   Caliban. Thou mak'st me merry: I am full of pleas-
      ure;
Let us be jocund. Will you troll the catch
You taught me but whilere?   124
   Stephano. At thy request, monster, I will do reason,

102 utensils stressed ´ — ´. 103 **deck withal** furnish it with.
104 **that** that which is. 123 **troll the catch** sing the song; a catch
was 'a round in which one singer catches at the words of another,
producing ludicrous effects' (OED). 124 **whilere** a while ago.

any reason. Come on, Trinculo, let us sing.   *Sings.*

> *Flout 'em and scout 'em—and scout 'em and flout 'em;*
> *Thought is free.*

Caliban. That's not the tune.
                    Ariel plays the tune on a tabor and pipe.
Stephano. What is this same?   130
Trinculo. This is the tune of our catch, play'd by
the picture of No-body.
Stephano. If thou beest a man, show thyself in thy
likeness: if thou beest a divel, take't as thou list.
Trinculo. O forgive me my sins.   135
Stephano. He that dies pays all debts. I defy thee;
mercy upon us!
Caliban. Art thou afeard?
Stephano. No, monster, not I.
Caliban. Be not afeard, the isle is full of noises,   140
Sounds and sweet airs that give delight and hurt not.
Sometimes a thousand twangling instruments
Will hum about mine ears, and sometime voices
That if I then had wak'd after long sleep
Will make me sleep again; and then in dreaming 145
The clouds methought would open and show riches
Ready to drop upon me, that when I wak'd
I cried to dream again.
Stephano. This will prove a brave kingdom to me,
where I shall have my music for nothing.   150
Caliban. When Prospero is destroy'd.
Stephano. That shall be by and by: I remember the
story.

---

127 scout F prints *cout* the first time, *scout* the second. SD **tabor**
small drum. 132 **picture of No-body** N. 140 **noises** music.

Trinculo. The sound is going away. Let's follow it
and after do our work.   155
 Stephano. Lead, monster, we'll follow. I would I
could see this taborer; he lays it on.
 Trinculo. Wilt come? I'll follow, Stephano. *Exeunt.*

SCENE 3

*Enter Alonso, Sebastian, Antonio, Gonzalo, Adrian,
Francisco, etc.*

 Gonzalo. By'r lakin, I can go no further, sir.
My old bones aches; here's a maze trod indeed
Through forthrights and meanders; by your pa-
    tience,
I needs must rest me.
 Alonso.   Old lord, I cannot blame thee
Who am myself attach'd with weariness   5
To th' dulling of my spirits; sit down and rest.
Even here I will put off my hope and keep it
No longer for my flatterer: he is drown'd
Whom thus we stray to find and the sea mocks
Our frustrate search on land. Well, let him go.   10
 Antonio. [*To Sebastian.*] I am right glad that he's
    so out of hope.
Do not for one repulse forgo the purpose
That you resolv'd t' effect.

1 **lakin** Ladykin (the Virgin Mary). 2 **aches** old variant plural
form of verb. 3 **forthrights** straight paths. **meanders** winding
paths. 5 **attach'd** seized. 6 **To th'** to the point of. **spirits** vital
strength. 10 **frustrate** vain.

Sebastian.   The next advantage
Will we take throughly.

Antonio.   Let it be tonight,
For now they are oppress'd with travel, they   15
Will not nor cannot use such vigilance
As when they are fresh.

Sebastian.   I say tonight: no more.

Solemn and strange music, and Prosper on the top,
invisible.

Alonso. What harmony is this? My good friends,
      hark!

Gonzalo. Marvelous sweet music.

Enter several strange shapes bringing in a banket;
and dance about it with gentle actions of salutations,
and inviting the king, etc. to eat, they depart.

Alonso. Give us kind keepers, heavens! What were
      these?   20

Sebastian. A living drollery! Now I will believe
That there are unicorns! that in Arabia
There is one tree, the phoenix' throne, one phoenix
At this hour reigning there.

Antonio.   I'll believe both!
And what does else want credit, come to me   25
And I'll be sworn 'tis true! Travelers nere did lie,
Though fools at home condemn 'em.

Gonzalo.   If in Naples
I should report this now, would they believe me?
If I should say I saw such islanders—
For certes these are people of the island—   30
Who though they are of monstrous shape yet, note,

14 **throughly** thoroughly. SD **Prosper on the top** N. 20 **keepers**
guardian angels. 21 **drollery** puppet show. 23 **phoenix** N. 29 **is-**
landers F *islands.*

60

Their manners are more gentle, kind, than of
Our human generation you shall find
Many, nay almost any.
  Prospero. [*Aside.*]   Honest lord,   34
Thou hast said well: for some of you there present
Are worse than divels.
  Alonso.   I cannot too much muse
Such shapes, such gesture, and such sound express-
     ing—
Although they want the use of tongue—a kind
Of excellent dumb discourse.
  Prospero. [*Aside.*]   Praise in departing.   39
  Francisco. They vanish'd strangely.
  Sebastian.   No matter, since
They have left their viands behind, for we have
     stomachs.
Will't please you taste of what is here?
  Alonso.   Not I.
  Gonzalo. Faith, sir, you need not fear! When we
     were boys
Who would believe that there were mountaineers
Dewlapp'd like bulls, whose throats had hanging at
     'em   45
Wallets of flesh? or that there were such men
Whose heads stood in their breasts? which now we
     find
Each putter out of five for one will bring us
Good warrant of.
  Alonso.   I will stand to and feed.
Although my last, no matter, since I feel   50

36 **muse** marvel at. 37 **gesture** bearing. 39 **Praise in departing**
proverbial: 'Wait until the end of the entertainment before you
praise it.' 48 **putter . . . one** N.

The best is past: brother, my lord the duke,
Stand to and do as we.

Thunder and lightning. Enter Ariel like a harpy,
claps his wings upon the table, and with a quaint
device the banquet vanishes.

Ariel. You are three men of sin, whom destiny—
That hath to instrument this lower world
And what is in't—the never surfeited sea   55
Hath caus'd to belch up you, and on this island
Where man doth not inhabit, you 'mongst men
Being most unfit to live; I have made you mad,
And even with such-like valor men hang and drown
Their proper selves.

                    [*Alonso, etc., draw their swords.*]
              You fools! I and my fellows   60
Are ministers of fate; the elements
Of whom your swords are temper'd may as well
Wound the loud winds, or with bemock'd-at stabs
Kill the still closing waters as diminish   64
One dowl that's in my plume! My fellow ministers
Are like invulnerable—if you could hurt,
Your swords are now too massy for your strengths
And will not be uplifted. But remember—
For that's my business to you—that you three
From Milan did supplant good Prospero,   70
Expos'd unto the sea—which hath requit it—
Him and his innocent child; for which foul deed
The powers, delaying—not forgetting—have
Incens'd the seas and shores, yea all the creatures

SD **quaint** ingenious. **the banquet vanishes** i.e. under the conceal-
ment of Ariel's wings (cf. *Aeneid* III.225–66). 54 **hath to instrument** uses for its own ends. 55 **surfeited** N. 60 **proper** own. 65 **dowl**
feather. **ministers** agents. 71 **requit it** retaliated (by wrecking
Alonso and his party).

Against your peace: thee of thy son, Alonso,   75
They have bereft and do pronounce by me:
Ling'ring perdition—worse than any death
Can be at once—shall step by step attend
You and your ways, whose wraths to guard you
    from—
Which here in this most desolate isle else falls   80
Upon your heads—is nothing but heart's sorrow
And a clear life ensuing.

*He vanishes in thunder; then, to soft music, enter the
shapes again and dance, with mocks and mows, and
carrying out the table.*

  Prospero. Bravely the figure of this harpy hast thou
Perform'd, my Ariel; a grace it had, devouring.
Of my instruction hast thou nothing bated   85
In what thou hadst to say. So with good life
And observation strange my meaner ministers
Their several kinds have done, my high charms work,
And these, mine enemies, are all knit up
In their distractions; they now are in my power, 90
And in these fits I leave them, while I visit
Young Ferdinand—whom they suppose is drown'd—
And his and mine lov'd darling.   [*Exit.*]
  Gonzalo. I' th' name of something holy, sir, why
    stand you
In this strange stare?
  Alonso.   O, it is monstrous! monstrous!
Methought the billows spoke and told me of it;   96
The winds did sing it to me, and the thunder—
That deep and dreadful organ pipe—pronounc'd

82 **clear** blameless. SD **mows** grimaces. 83 **bravely** admirably.
84 **devouring** i.e. pretending to eat the food of the banquet.
85 **bated** omitted. 86 **with good life** like real life.

The name of Prosper! It did bass my trespass.
Therefore my son i' th' ooze is bedded, and　　　100
I'll seek him deeper than ere plummet sounded,
And with him there lie mudded.　　　　　　*Exit.*
　　Sebastian.　　　　　　But one fiend at a
　　　　time—
I'll fight their legions ore!
　　Antonio.　　　　　　　I'll be thy second.
　　　　　　Exeunt [Sebastian and Antonio].
　　Gonzalo. All three of them are desperate! Their
　　　　great guilt,
Like poison given to work a great time after,　　105
Now 'gins to bite the spirits. I do beseech you,
That are of suppler joints, follow them swiftly
And hinder them from what this ecstasy
May now provoke them to.
　　Adrian.　　　　　　Follow, I pray you.
　　　　　　　　　Exeunt omnes.

99 **bass** sang the bass harmony of nature's dirge. 106 **bite the**
spirits impair the vital powers. 108 **ecstasy** madness.

64

Act IV

SCENE 1

Enter Prospero, Ferdinand, and Miranda.

Prospero. If I have too austerely punish'd you
Your compensation makes amends, for I
Have given you here a third of mine own life,
Or that for which I live, who once again
I tender to thy hand; all thy vexations   5
Were but my trials of thy love, and thou
Hast strangely stood the test. Here, afore heaven,
I ratify this my rich gift! O Ferdinand,
Do not smile at me that I boast her off,
For thou shalt find she will outstrip all praise   10
And make it halt behind her.

Ferdinand.   I do believe it
Against an oracle.

Prospero. Then as my gift and thine own acquisition
Worthily purchas'd, take my daughter; but
If thou dost break her virgin knot before   15
All sanctimonious ceremonies may
With full and holy rite be minist'red,
No sweet aspersion shall the heavens let fall
To make this contract grow, but barren hate,
Sour-ey'd disdain, and discord shall bestrew   20

3 **third** N. 7 **strangely** surprisingly well. 9 **boast her off** cf. the
modern 'show her off'; F *of*. 11 **halt** limp. 13 **gift** F *guest*. 16 **sanc-timonious** holy. 17 **rite** F *right*. 18 **aspersion** sprinkling of the dew
of blessing.

The union of your bed with weeds so loathly
That you shall hate it both. Therefore take heed
As Hymen's lamps shall light you.

Ferdinand.   As I hope
For quiet days, fair issue, and long life
With such love as 'tis now, the murkiest den,   25
The most opportune place, the strong'st suggestion
Our worser genius can, shall never melt
Mine honor into lust, to take away
The edge of that day's celebration   29
When I shall think or Phoebus' steeds are founder'd,
Or Night kept chain'd below.

Prospero.   Fairly spoke.
Sit then and talk with her; she is thine own.

                                   [*They sit apart.*]
What, Ariel! my industrious servant, Ariel!

Enter Ariel.

Ariel. What would my potent master? Here I am.

Prospero. Thou and thy meaner fellows your last
    service   35
Did worthily perform, and I must use you
In such another trick. Go bring the rabble—
Ore whom I give thee power—here to this place.
Incite them to quick motion, for I must
Bestow upon the eyes of this young couple   40
Some vanity of mine art: it is my promise
And they expect it from me.

Ariel.   Presently?

Prospero. Ay, with a twinck.

26 **opportune** stressed $- \cup -$. 27 **worser genius** N. 28 **to** so as to.
29 **edge** keen enjoyment. 30 **Phoebus'** Apollo, god of the sun.
founder'd gone lame. 30–1 **or . . . below** i.e. eternal day, time
standing still. 37 **trick** ingenious piece of mechanism (Arden ed.).
41 **vanity** illusion. 42 **Presently** immediately.

Ariel. Before you can say 'come' and 'go,'
And breathe twice, and cry 'so, so,'   45
Each one tripping on his toe
Will be here with mop and mow
Do you love me, master? no?

Prospero. Dearly, my delicate Ariel! Do not ap-
    proach   49
Till thou dost hear me call.

Ariel.   Well! I conceive.   *Exit.*

Prospero. [*Back to Ferdinand.*] Look thou be true:
    do not give dalliance
Too much the reign; the strongest oaths are straw
To th' fire i' th' blood. Be more abstemious,
Or else good night your vow.

Ferdinand.   I warrant you, sir,
The white cold virgin snow upon my heart   55
Abates the ardor of my liver.

Prospero.   Well.
Now come, my Ariel, bring a corollary
Rather than want a spirit; appear, and pertly.
No tongue—all eyes—be silent.

Soft music. Enter Iris.

Iris. Ceres, most bounteous lady, thy rich leas   60
Of wheat, rye, barley, fetches, oats, and peas;
Thy turfy mountains where live nibbling sheep,
And flat meads thetch'd with stover, them to keep;

---

47 mop and mow grimaces. **50 conceive** understand. **56 liver**
popularly supposed to be the origin of the love passions. **57 corol-**
lary extra spirit. **58 pertly** promptly. **60 Iris** messenger of the
gods, uniting gods and man. **Ceres** goddess of agriculture and
marriage. **61 fetches** 'vetch,' a leguminous plant. **63 thetch'd**
thatched. **stover** fodder. **keep** provide with fodder.

67

Thy banks with pioned and twilled brims
Which spongy April at thy hest betrims   65
To make cold nymphs chaste crowns; and thy broom
      groves
Whose shadow the dismissed bachelor loves,
Being lass-lorn; thy poll-clipp'd vineyard;
And thy sea-marge stirrile and rocky-hard,   69
Where thou thyself dost air—the queen o' th' sky,
Whose wat'ry arch and messenger am I,
Bids thee leave these and with her sovereign grace
                              Juno [begins to] descend.
Here on this grass plot in this very place
To come and sport. Her peacocks fly amain.
Approach, rich Ceres, her to entertain.   75

Enter Ceres.

Ceres. Hail, many-color'd messenger, that nere
Dost disobey the wife of Jupiter;
Who with thy saffron wings upon my flowers
Diffusest honey drops, refreshing showers,
And with each end of thy blue bow dost crown   80
My bosky acres and my unshrubb'd down,
Rich scarf to my proud earth—why hath thy queen
Summon'd me hither to this short-grass'd green?
Iris. A contract of true love to celebrate
And some donation freely to estate   85
On the bless'd lovers.

64 **pioned and twilled** N. 65 **hest** command. 66 **broom** a flowering
shrub. 68 **poll-clipp'd** F *pole-clipt.* **vineyard** here trisyllabic. 69
stirrile sterile. 71 **wat'ry arch** rainbow. **messenger** Iris was the
particular messenger of Juno as well as a personification of the
rainbow. 72 **grace** majesty. SD **Juno . . . descend** N. 74 **amain**
in full force. 80 **bow** rainbow. 81 **bosky** bushy. **unshrubb'd down**
rolling, treeless hills. 85 **estate** bestow.

Ceres.   Tell me, heavenly bow,
If Venus or her son, as thou dost know,
Do now attend the queen? Since they did plot
The means that dusky Dis my daughter got,
Her and her blind boy's scandal'd company   90
I have forsworn.
  Iris.   Of her society
Be not afraid; I met her deity
Cutting the clouds towards Paphos, and her son
Dove-drawn with her. Here thought they to have done
Some wanton charm upon this man and maid   95
Whose vows are that no bedrite shall be paid
Till Hymen's torch be lighted; but in vain:
Mars's hot minion is return'd again;
Her waspish-headed son has broke his arrows,   99
Swears he will shoot no more but play with sparrows
And be a boy right out.
  Ceres.   Highest queen of state,
Great Juno comes; I know her by her gait.

[*Enter Juno.*]

Juno. How does my bounteous sister? Go with me
To bless this twain, that they may prosperous be 104
And honor'd in their issue.   *They sing.*

[Song]

  Juno.   *Honor, riches, marriage, blessing,*
            Long continuance and increasing,

89 **that** by which. **Dis** Pluto, who stole Proserpine, Ceres' daughter. 90 **blind boy's** Cupid's. **scandal'd** scandalous. 93 **Paphos** one of the seats of worship of Venus. 96 **bedrite** F *bed-right*. 98 **Mars's hot minion** Venus was the mistress of Mars; F *Marses*. 99 **waspish-headed** spiteful. 100. **sparrows** associated with worship of Venus. 102 **gait** royal walk. 104 **prosperous** a pun on 'Prospero's' is possible.

> Hourly joys, be still upon you,
> Juno sings her blessings on you.
>
> *Ceres.* Earth's increase, foison plenty,   110
> Barns and garners never empty,
> Vines with clust'ring bunches growing,
> Plants with goodly burthen bowing:
> Spring come to you at the farthest
> In the very end of harvest!   115
> Scarcity and want shall shun you;
> Ceres' blessing so is on you.

Ferdinand. This is a most majestic vision and
Harmonious charmingly; may I be bold   119
To think these spirits?
   Prospero.   Spirits which by mine art
I have from their confines call'd to enact
My present fancies.
   Ferdinand.   Let me live here ever!
So rare a wond'red father and a wise
Makes this place paradise.

    Juno and Ceres whisper, and send Iris on
          employment.

   Prospero.   Sweet now, silence.
Juno and Ceres whisper seriously.   125
There's something else to do—hush and be mute
Or else our spell is marr'd.
   Iris. You nymphs, call'd naiads, of the windring
      brooks,

108 **still** always. 110 **Ceres** speech ascription omitted in F. **Earth's**
here disyllabic (read 'earthes'). **foison** abundance of harvest.
114 **Spring . . . farthest** i.e. eliminating winter. 119 **charmingly**
magically. 123 **wond'red** possessing wonder; cf. 'bearded,' 'blue-
eyed,' etc. (Kittredge). SD **Juno . . . employment** F places this
after l. 127. 124 **Sweet . . . silence** to Miranda, who is about to
speak. 128 **windring** perhaps a combination of 'winding' and
'wandering.'

With your sedg'd crowns and ever-harmless looks,
Leave your crisp channels and on this green land   130
Answer your summons; Juno does command.
Come, temperate nymphs, and help to celebrate
A contract of true love: be not too late.

Enter certain nymphs.

You sunburn'd sicklemen of August weary,
Come hither from the furrow and be merry;   135
Make holiday, your rye-straw hats put on,
And these fresh nymphs encounter every one
In country footing.

*Enter certain reapers, properly habited. They join
with the nymphs in a graceful dance, towards the end
whereof Prospero starts suddenly and speaks, after
which, to a strange hollow and confused noise, they
heavily vanish.*

  Prospero. [*Aside.*] I had forgot that foul con-
    spiracy
Of the beast Caliban and his confederates   140
Against my life. The minute of their plot
Is almost come. [*To spirits.*] Well done, avoid! no
    more.
  Ferdinand. This is strange! Your father's in some
    passion
That works him strongly.
  Miranda.   Never till this day
Saw I him touch'd with anger so distemper'd.   145
  Prospero. You do look, my son, in a mov'd sort,
As if you were dismay'd—be cheerful, sir.

130 crisp rippling. land N. 132 temperate chaste. 138 footing
dancing. 142 avoid be gone. 145 distemper'd unbalanced, dis-
turbed. 146 sort manner.

Our revels now are ended: these our actors—
As I foretold you—were all spirits and
Are melted into air, into thin air;   150
And like the baseless fabric of this vision
The cloud-capp'd towers, the gorgeous palaces,
The solemn temples, the great globe itself,
Yea, all which it inherit, shall dissolve
And like this insubstantial pageant faded   155
Leave not a rack behind: we are such stuff
As dreams are made on, and our little life
Is rounded with a sleep. Sir, I am vex'd;
Bear with my weakness, my old brain is troubled!
Be not disturb'd with my infirmity.   160
If you be pleas'd, retire into my cell
And there repose; a turn or two I'll walk
To still my beating mind.
   Ferdinand. Miranda.   We wish your peace.

                         Exeunt.

   Prospero. Come with a thought! I thank thee, Ariel:
   Come!

Enter Ariel.

   Ariel. Thy thoughts I cleave to. What's thy
   pleasure?
   Prospero.   Spirit,   165
We must prepare to meet with Caliban.
   Ariel. Ay, my commander. When I presented Ceres
I thought to have told thee of it, but I fear'd
Lest I might anger thee.

154 **it inherit** possess it. 156 **rack** moving cloud, with a possible
double meaning ('wrack'). 157 **on** of. 158 **rounded with** 'rounded
off by,' or perhaps 'surrounded by.' 163 **beating** overwrought.
164 **Come . . . thought** be summoned by mental telepathy.
thank thee spoken to Ariel before he appears. 167 **presented**
enacted. 168 **to have** read 't'have.'

    72

Prospero. Say again, where didst thou leave these
    varlets? 170
  Ariel. I told you, sir, they were red hot with drink-
    ing,
So full of valor that they smote the air
For breathing in their faces, beat the ground
For kissing of their feet, yet always bending
Towards their project. Then I beat my tabor, 175
At which like unback'd colts they prick'd their ears
Advanc'd their eyelids, lifted up their noses
As they smelt music; so I charm'd their ears
That calflike they my lowing follow'd, through
Tooth'd briers, sharp furzes, pricking goss, and
    thorns, 180
Which ent'red their frail shins. At last I left them
I' th' filthy-mantled pool beyond your cell,
There dancing up to th' chins, that the foul lake
Orestunk their feet.
  Prospero.   This was well done, my bird.
Thy shape invisible retain thou still. 185
The trumpery in my house, go bring it hither
For stale to catch these thieves.
  Ariel.   I go, I go.   *Exit.*
  Prospero. A devil, a born devil, on whose nature
Nurture can never stick, on whom my pains,
Humanely taken, all, all lost, quite lost, 190
And, as with age, his body uglier grows,
So his mind cankers. I will plague them all,
Even to roaring!

---

176 **unback'd** unbroken. 180 **goss** gorse. 182 **filthy-mantled** sur-
faced with dirty scum. 186 **trumpery** trash, rubbish. 187 **stale**
decoy. 193 **hang . . . on** F *hang on them;* in F this speech pre-
cedes SD. line N.

Enter Ariel, loaden with glistering apparel, etc.

Come, hang them on this line.

Enter Caliban, Stephano, and Trinculo, all wet.

Caliban. Pray you, tread softly, that the blind mole
may not hear a footfall: we are now near his cell. 195

Stephano. Monster, your fairy, which you say is a
harmless fairy, has done little better than play'd the
Jack with us.

Trinculo. Monster, I do smell all horse piss, at which
my nose is in great indignation. 200

Stephano. So is mine. Do you hear, monster: If I
should take a displeasure against you—look you.

Trinculo. Thou wert but a lost monster.

Caliban. Good my lord, give me thy favor still.
Be patient, for the prize I'll bring thee to 205
Shall hoodwink this mischance. Therefore speak
        softly;
All's hush'd as midnight yet.

Trinculo. Ay, but to lose our bottles in the pool!

Stephano. There is not only disgrace and dishonor
in that, monster, but an infinite loss. 210

Trinculo. That's more to me than my wetting! Yet
this is your harmless fairy, monster.

Stephano. I will fetch off my bottle, though I be ore
ears for my labor. 214

Caliban. Prithee, my king, be quiet. Seest thou here,
This is the mouth o' th' cell! no noise and enter.
Do that good mischief which may make this island
Thine own for ever and I thy Caliban
For aye thy foot-licker. 219

---

198 **Jack** knave. 206 **hoodwink . . . mischance** 'blind you to
this misfortune'; the reference is to falconry; F *hudwinke.*

Stephano. Give me thy hand. I do begin to have
bloody thoughts.

Trinculo. O King Stephano, O peer! O worthy
Stephano! Look what a wardrobe here is for thee!

Caliban. Let it alone, thou fool, it is but trash. 224

Trinculo. Oho, monster! We know what belongs to
a frippery. O King Stephano!

Stephano. Put off that gown, Trinculo. By this
hand, *I'll* have that gown!

Trinculo. Thy grace shall have it.

Caliban. The dropsy drown this fool! What do you
     mean   230
To dote thus on such luggage? Let's alone
And do the murther first: if he awake,
From toe to crown he'll fill our skins with pinches.
Make us strange stuff.   234

Stephano. Be you quiet, monster! Mistress line, is
not this my jerkin? Now is the jerkin under the line!
Now, jerkin, you are like to lose your hair and prove
a bald jerkin.

Trinculo. Do, do; we steal by line and level, and't
like your grace.   240

Stephano. I thank thee for that jest; here's a garment for't: wit shall not go unrewarded while I am
king of this country! 'Steal by line and level' is an
excellent pass of pate! There's another garment for't.

---

222 O . . . peer N. 226 **frippery** old clothes shop. 231 **luggage**
encumbrance. **Let's alone** let us leave it alone (or perhaps *let's*
is a misprint for 'let't', or *alone* a misprint for 'along'). 234 **strange
stuff** different cloth (metaphorically, continuing the idea of
frippery in l. 226). 235–8 **Mistress . . . bald jerkin** N. 239 **we
. . . level** N. **and't like** if it please. 244 **pass of pate** rapier thrust
of wit, sally.

Trinculo. Monster, come put some lime upon your fingers, and away with the rest.   246

Caliban. I will have none on't—we shall lose our time
And all be turn'd to barnacles or to apes
With foreheads villainous low.   249

Stephano. Monster, lay-to your fingers! Help to bear this away where my hogshead of wine is, or I'll turn you out of my kingdom! Go to, carry this.

Trinculo. And this.

Stephano. Ay, and this.

A noise of hunters heard. Enter divers spirits in shape of dogs and hounds, hunting them about, Prospero and Ariel setting them on.

Prospero. Hey, Mountain, hey!   255
Ariel. Silver! There it goes, Silver!
Prospero. Fury, Fury! There, Tyrant, there! Hark, hark!   [*Exeunt all but Prospero and Ariel.*]
Go charge my goblins that they grind their joints
With dry convulsions, shorten up their sinews
With aged cramps, and more pinch-spotted make them   260
Than pard or cat-o'-mountain.
Ariel.   Hark, they roar!
Prospero. Let them be hunted soundly! At this hour
Lies at my mercy all mine enemies!
Shortly shall all my labors end, and thou
Shalt have the air at freedom! For a little   265
Follow, and do me service.   *Exeunt.*

245 lime N. 248 **barnacles** probably the barnacle goose, thought to hatch from a sea shell. 261 **pard** leopard. **cat-o'-mountain** catamount, lynx.

Act V

SCENE 1

Enter Prospero in his magic robes, and Ariel.

Prospero. Now does my project gather to a head;
My charms crack not, my spirits obey, and Time
Goes upright with his carriage. How's the day?

Ariel. On the sixt hour, at which time, my lord,
You said our work should cease.

Prospero.   I did say so   5
When first I rais'd the tempest. Say, my spirit,
How fares the king and's followers?

Ariel.   Confin'd
        together
In the same fashion as you gave in charge,
Just as you left them; all prisoners, sir,
In the line grove which weather-fends your cell;   10
They cannot budge till your release. The king,
His brother, and yours, abide all three distracted,
And the remainder mourning over them
Brimful of sorrow and dismay, but chiefly   14
Him that you term'd, sir, the good old lord, Gonzalo.
His tears runs down his beard like winter's drops
From eaves of reeds. Your charm so strongly works
        'em

3 Goes . . . **carriage** walks with erect carriage, instead of bow-
ing under his burden. **How's the day** what time is it? 10 **weather-
fends** protects from the weather. 11 **your release** released by you.
17 **reeds** a thatched roof.

That if you now beheld them, your affections
Would become tender.

Prospero.   Dost thou think so, spirit?
Ariel. Mine would, sir, were I human.

Prospero.   And mine
    shall.   20
Hast thou—which art but air—a touch, a feeling
Of their afflictions, and shall not myself,
One of their kind, that relish all as sharply,
Passion as they, be kindlier mov'd than thou art?
Though with their high wrongs I am struck to th'
    quick,   25
Yet with my nobler reason 'gainst my fury
Do I take part: the rarer action is
In virtue than in vengeance; they being penitent,
The sole drift of my purpose doth extend
Not a frown further. Go, release them, Ariel.   30
My charms I'll break, their senses I'll restore,
And they shall be themselves.

Ariel.   I'll fetch them, sir.

                                                       Exit.
Prospero. Ye elves of hills, brooks, standing lakes,
    and groves,
And ye that on the sands with printless foot
Do chase the ebbing Neptune and do fly him   35
When he comes back; you demipuppets that
By moonshine do the green sour ringlets make,
Whereof the ewe not bites; and you whose pastime

---

18 **affections** feelings. 21–4 N. 23 **all** fully. 27 **rarer** finer. 33–41 **Ye elves** . . . Prospero draws a circle on the ground as he calls upon the spirits; see SD below. 36 **demipuppets** half the size of puppets. 37 **green sour ringlets** 'the underground part (mycelium) of a toadstool, which affects the grass roots' (Arden ed.).

78

Is to make midnight mushrumps, that rejoice
To hear the solemn curfew, by whose aid,   40
Weak masters though ye be, I have bedimm'd
The noontide sun, call'd forth the mutinous winds,
And 'twixt the green sea and the azur'd vault
Set roaring war; to the dread, rattling thunder
Have I given fire, and rifted Jove's stout oak   45
With his own bolt; the strong-bas'd promontory
Have I made shake and by the spurs pluck'd up
The pine and cedar. Graves at my command
Have wak'd their sleepers, op'd and let 'em forth
By my so potent art. But this rough magic   50
I here abjure, and when I have requir'd
Some heavenly music—which even now I do—
To work mine end upon their senses, that
This airy charm is for, I'll break my staff,
Bury it certain fadoms in the earth,   55
And deeper than did ever plummet sound
I'll drown my book.

Solemn music. Here enters Ariel before, then Alonso,
with a frantic gesture, attended by Gonzalo; Sebas-
tian and Antonio in like manner attended by Adrian
and Francisco. They all enter the circle which Pros-
pero had made and there stand charm'd; which
Prospero observing, speaks.

A solemn air and the best comforter
To an unsettled fancy, cure thy brains,
Now useless, boil'd within thy skull; there stand,   60

39 **mushrumps** mushrooms. 53–4 their . . . **for** the senses of those
this airy charm is for. 54 **airy charm** play on two meanings of
airy ('of the air' and 'of music') and two of *charm* ('magic' and
'song'). 58 **air** melody. 59 **thy** Prospero addresses Alonso. 60
boil'd overwrought; F *boile*, probably a misprint of *e* for *d*.

For you are spell-stopp'd.
Holy Gonzalo, honorable man,
Mine eyes, ev'n sociable to the show of thine,
Fall fellowly drops. The charm dissolves apace,
And as the morning steals upon the night,   65
Melting the darkness, so their rising senses
Begin to chase the ignorant fumes that mantle
Their clearer reason. O good Gonzalo,
My true preserver and a loyal sir
To him thou follow'st! I will pay thy graces   70
Home both in word and deed. Most cruelly
Didst thou, Alonso, use me and my daughter.
Thy brother was a furtherer in the act.
Thou art pinch'd for't now, Sebastian. Flesh and
      blood,
You, brother mine, that entertain'd ambition,   75
Expell'd remorse and nature, who, with Sebastian—
Whose inward pinches, therefore, are most strong—
Would here have kill'd your king: I do forgive thee,
Unnatural though thou art. Their understanding
Begins to swell, and the approaching tide   80
Will shortly fill the reasonable shores
That now lie foul and muddy. Not one of them
That yet looks on me or would know me. Ariel,
Fetch me the hat and rapier in my cell.
I will discase me, and myself present   85
As I was sometime Milan—quickly, spirit!
Thou shalt ere long be free.

63 **sociable** sympathetic. **show** sight. 64 **Fall** let fall, shed.
67 **ignorant fumes** fumes that make them ignorant (oblivious).
70–1 **pay . . . Home** repay your kindness. 72 **Didst** F *Did*.
75 **entertain'd** was host to; F *entertaine*. 76 **who** F *whom*. 81 **shores**
i.e. of reason; F *shore*. 85 **discase** remove my magic robe. 86 **sometime** formerly. **Milan** Duke of Milan.

Ariel [after fetching the clothes] sings and helps to attire him.

[Song]

> Ariel. Where the bee sucks there suck I;
>   In a cowslip's bell I lie;
>   There I couch when owls do cry;   90
>   On the bat's back I do fly
>   After summer merrily.
>   Merrily, merrily shall I live now
>   Under the blossom that hangs on the bough.

Prospero. Why that's my dainty Ariel! I shall miss
    thee,   95
But yet thou shalt have freedom—so, so, so.
To the king's ship, invisible as thou art!
There shalt thou find the mariners asleep
Under the hatches. The master and the boatswain
Being awake, enforce them to this place,   100
And presently, I prithee.
    Ariel. I drink the air before me and return
Or ere your pulse twice beat.   *Exit.*
    Gonzalo. All torment, trouble, wonder, and amaze-
        ment
Inhabits here! Some heavenly power guide us   105
Out of this fearful country!
    Prospero.   Behold, Sir King,
The wronged Duke of Milan, Prospero!
For more assurance that a living prince
Does now speak to thee, I embrace thy body,
And to thee and thy company I bid   110
A hearty welcome.

---

92 **after** following after. 101 **presently** immediately. 103 **Or ere** before. 108 **For more assurance** to give you more proof.

Alonso.   Where thou beest he or no,
Or some enchanted trifle to abuse me—
As late I have been—I not know. Thy pulse
Beats as of flesh and blood, and since I saw thee
Th' affliction of my mind amends, with which   115
I fear a madness held me! This must crave—
And if this be at all—a most strange story.
Thy dukedom I resign and do entreat
Thou pardon me my wrongs. But how should Prospero
Be living and be here?
   Prospero.   First, noble friend,   120
Let me embrace thine age, whose honor cannot
Be measur'd or confin'd.
   Gonzalo.   Whether this be
Or be not I'll not swear.
   Prospero.   You do yet taste
Some subtleties o' th' isle, that will not let you
Believe things certain. Welcome, my friends all,   125
[*Aside to Sebastian and Antonio.*] But you, my brace
        of lords; were I so minded
I here could pluck his Highness' frown upon you
And justify you traitors! At this time
I will tell no tales.
   Sebastian.   The divel speaks in him!
   Prospero.   No!
For you, most wicked sir, whom to call brother   130
Would even infect my mouth, I do forgive
Thy rankest fault—all of them—and require
My dukedom of thee, which perforce I know
Thou must restore.

111 **Where** whether. 112 **enchanted trifle** unsubstantial spirit.
abuse deceive. 116 **crave** necessitate. 117 **And if** if. 121 **age** aged
body. 124 **subtleties** illusions, especially disguised confections.
125 **certain** real. 128 **justify** prove.

Alonso.   If thou beest Prospero
Give us particulars of thy preservation,   135
How thou hast met us here who three hours since
Were wrack'd upon this shore, where I have lost—
How sharp the point of this remembrance is—
My dear son Ferdinand.

Prospero.   I am woe for't, sir.

Alonso. Irreparable is the loss, and patience   140
Says it is past her cure.

Prospero.   I rather think
You have not sought her help, of whose soft grace
For the like loss I have her sovereign aid,
And rest myself content.

Alonso.   You the like loss?   144

Prospero. As great to me as late, and supportable
To make the dear loss have I means much weaker
Than you may call to comfort you, for I
Have lost my daughter.

Alonso.   A daughter?
O heavens that they were living both in Naples,   149
The king and queen there; that they were I wish
Myself were mudded in that oozy bed
Where my son lies! When did you lose your daughter?

Prospero. In this last tempest. I perceive these lords
At this encounter do so much admire
That they devour their reason and scarce think   155
Their eyes do offices of truth; their words
Are natural breath; but howsoe'er you have
Been justled from your senses, know for certain
That I am Prospero and that very duke   159

136 who F *whom.* 139 **am woe for't** grieve because of it. 140 **patience** fortitude. 142 **grace** mercy. 145 **late** recent. **supportable** stressed $\smile - \smile -$. 146 **dear** great. 150 **that** provided that. 154 **admire** marvel. 155 **devour their reason** their reason is swallowed up by amazement.

Which was thrust forth of Milan, who most strangely
Upon this shore, where you were wrack'd, was landed
To be the lord on't. No more yet of this,
For 'tis a chronicle of day by day,
Not a relation for a breakfast, nor
Befitting this first meeting. Welcome, sir.   165
This cell's my court; here have I few attendants,
And subjects none abroad; pray you look in.
My dukedom since you have given me again
I will requite you with as good a thing,
At least bring forth a wonder to content ye   170
As much as me my dukedom.

*Here Prospero discovers Ferdinand and Miranda,
playing at chess.*

Miranda. Sweet lord, you play me false.

Ferdinand.   No, my
     dearest love,
I would not for the world.

Miranda. Yes, for a score of kingdoms you should
     wrangle,
And I would call it fair play.

Alonso.   If this prove   175
A vision of the island, one dear son
Shall I twice lose.

Sebastian.   A most high miracle.

Ferdinand. [*Seeing Alonso.*] Though the seas
     threaten, they are merciful.
I have curs'd them without cause.

Alonso.   Now all the bless-
     ings
Of a glad father compass thee about!   180
Arise and say how thou cam'st here.

SD Prospero pulls aside the curtain to the inner stage. 174–5 **Yes
. . . play** N.

84

Miranda.   O wonder!
How many goodly creatures are there here!
How beauteous mankind is! O brave new world
That has such people in't.
  Prospero.   'Tis new to thee.
  Alonso. What is this maid, with whom thou wast at
    play?   185
Your eld'st acquaintance cannot be three hours!
Is she the goddess that hath sever'd us
And brought us thus together?
  Ferdinand.   Sir, she is mortal,
But by immortal Providence she's mine.
I chose her when I could not ask my father   190
For his advice—nor thought I had one. She
Is daughter to this famous Duke of Milan,
Of whom so often I have heard renown
But never saw before, of whom I have
Receiv'd a second life; and second father   195
This lady makes him to me.
  Alonso.   I am hers.
But O, how oddly will it sound that I
Must ask my child forgiveness?
  Prospero.   There, sir, stop.
Let us not burthen our remembrance with
A heaviness that's gone.
  Gonzalo.   I have inly wept,   200
Or should have spoke ere this. Look down, you gods,
And on this couple drop a blessed crown,
For it is you that have chalk'd forth the way
Which brought us hither.
  Alonso.   I say amen, Gonzalo.

186 **eld'st** longest. 193 **renown** excellent report. 196 **am hers**
accept her as my daughter. 199 **remembrance** F *remembrances;*
see I.2.173 N.

Gonzalo. Was Milan thrust from Milan, that his
    issue   205
Should become kings of Naples? O rejoice
Beyond a common joy, and set it down
With gold on lasting pillars: in one voyage
Did Claribel her husband find at Tunis,
And Ferdinand her brother found a wife   210
Where he himself was lost; Prospero his dukedom
In a poor isle; and all of us ourselves,
When no man was his own.
    Alonso.   Give me your hands.
Let grief and sorrow still embrace his heart
That doth not wish you joy.
    Gonzalo.   Be it so, amen.   215

*Enter Ariel, with the Master and Boatswain amazedly
following.*

O look, sir, look, sir, here is more of us!
I prophesied if a gallows were on land
This fellow could not drown! Now, blasphemy,
That swear'st grace oreboard, not an oath on shore?
Hast thou no mouth by land? What is the news?   220
    Boatswain. The best news is that we have safely
    found
Our king and company; the next, our ship
Which but three glasses since we gave out split
Is tight and yare, and bravely rigg'd as when
We first put out to sea.
    Ariel.   Sir, all this service   225
Have I done since I went.
    Prospero.   My tricksy spirit!

213 **his own** master of himself. 214 **still** always. SD **amazedly**
as in a maze. 223 **but three glasses since** only three hours ago.
224 **yare** ready. 226 **tricksy** brisk.

Alonso. These are not natural events, they
    strengthen
From strange to stranger! Say, how came you hither?
  Boatswain. If I did think, sir, I were well awake,
I'd strive to tell you! We were dead of sleep   230
And—how we know not—all clapp'd under hatches,
Where, but even now, with strange and several noises
Of roaring, shrieking, howling, jingling chains,
And mo diversity of sounds, all horrible,
We were awak'd—straightway at liberty,   235
Where we, in all our trim, freshly beheld
Our royal, good, and gallant ship, our master
Cap'ring to eye her. On a trice, so please you,
Even in a dream, were we divided from them   239
And were brought moping hither.
  Ariel.   Was't well done?
  Prospero. Bravely, my diligence; thou shalt be free.
  Alonso. This is as strange a maze as ere men trod,
And there is in this business more than nature
Was ever conduct of! Some oracle
Must rectify our knowledge.
  Prospero.   Sir, my liege,   245
Do not infest your mind with beating on
The strangeness of this business; at pick'd leisure,
Which shall be shortly, single I'll resolve you—
Which to you shall seem probable—of every
These happen'd accidents; till when be cheerful   250
And think of each thing well. Come hither, spirit.

---

230 **of sleep** asleep. 232 **several** distinct. 234 **mo** more. 236 **our
trim** N. 238 **On** in. 240 **moping** bewildered. 241 **diligence** industrious one. 244 **conduct** conductor. 246 **infest** annoy. 247 **at pick'd
leisure** at a free moment we will choose. 248 **single** privately.
249 **every** every one of.

Set Caliban and his companions free:
Untie the spell.   [*Exit Ariel.*]
                        How fares my gracious sir?
There are yet missing of your company
Some few odd lads that you remember not.   255

> *Enter Ariel, driving in Caliban, Stephano, and*
> *Trinculo in their stolne apparel.*

Stephano. Every man shift for all the rest, and let
no man take care for himself, for all is but fortune
—*coragio*, bully-monster, *coragio!*
Trinculo. If these be true spies which I wear in my
head, here's a goodly sight.   260
Caliban. O Setebos, these be brave spirits indeed!
How fine my master is! I am afraid
He will chastise me.
Sebastian.   Ha ha!
What things are these, my Lord Antonio?
Will money buy 'em?
Antonio.   Very like! One of them   265
Is a plain fish and no doubt marketable.
Prospero. Mark but the badges of these men, my
        lords,
Then say if they be true. This misshapen knave
His mother was a witch and one so strong   269
That could control the moon, make flows and ebbs,
And deal in her command without her pow'r.
These three have robb'd me, and this demi-divel,

---

255 **few odd** several. 258 **coragio** courage. **bully-monster** good
fellow of a monster. 267 **badges** N. 268–9 **knave His mother**
knave's mother. 270 **flows** tides. 271 **deal . . . power** do all the
moon could do without assistance from the moon. 272 **demi-
divel** half a devil (offspring of a witch and the devil Setebos).

For he's a bastard one, had plotted with them
To take my life. Two of these fellows you
Must know and own, this thing of darkness I   275
Acknowledge mine.

   Caliban.   I shall be pinch'd to death.

   Alonso. Is not this Stephano, my drunken butler?

   Sebastian. He is drunk now; where had he wine?

   Alonso. And Trinculo is reeling ripe! Where should
      they
Find this grand liquor that hath gilded 'em?   280
How cam'st thou in this pickle?

   Trinculo. I have bin in such a pickle since I saw
you last that I fear me will never out of my bones; I
shall not fear fly-blowing.

   Sebastian. Why, how now Stephano?   285

   Stephano. O touch me not! I am not Stephano but
a cramp.

   Prospero. You'd be king o' the isle, sirrah?

   Stephano. I should have been a sore one then.   289

   Alonso. This is a strange thing as ere I look'd on.

   Prospero. He is as disproportion'd in his manners
As in his shape! Go, sirrah, to my cell;
Take with you your companions—as you look
To have my pardon, trim it handsomely.   294

   Caliban. Ay, that I will! and I'll be wise hereafter
And seek for grace! What a thrice-double ass

279 **reeling ripe** ripe (ready) for reeling. 280 **gilded** common term
for 'made drunk'—but in combination with 'grand liquor' probably also a play on the alchemical elixir which was supposed to
turn base metals to gold. 281 **pickle** drunken state. 282 **pickle**
brine, in reference to the dousing in the horse pond. 283 **that** as.
283–4 **I . . . fly-blowing** i.e. because he was so pickled, flies
would not touch him. 289 **sore** a pun: 'causing pain' and 'feeling
pain.'

Was I to take this drunkard for a god
And worship this dull fool!

Prospero.   Go to, away!

Alonso. Hence, and bestow your luggage where you
    found it.

Sebastian. Or stole it, rather.   300

       [*Exeunt Caliban, Stephano, and Trinculo.*]

Prospero. Sir, I invite your Highness and your
    train

To my poor cell, where you shall take your rest
For this one night, which, part of it, I'll waste
With such discourse as I not doubt shall make it
Go quick away: the story of my life   305
And the particular accidents gone by
Since I came to this isle; and in the morn
I'll bring you to your ship, and so to Naples,
Where I have hope to see the nuptial
Of these our dear belov'd solemnized,   310
And thence retire me to my Milan, where
Every third thought shall be my grave.

Alonso.   I long
To hear the story of your life, which must
Take the ear strangely.

Prospero.   I'll deliver all,
And promise you calm seas, auspicious gales,   315
And sail so expeditious that shall catch
Your royal fleet far off. My Ariel, chick,
That is thy charge—then to the elements
Be free, and fare thou well! Please you, draw near.

                            Exeunt omnes.

---

306 **accidents** incidents. 310 **solemnized** stressed — ´ — ˋ.
314 **deliver** relate.
   90

Epilogue

Spoken by Prospero

Now my charms are all o'erthrown,
And what strength I have's mine own,
Which is most faint. Now, 'tis true,
I must be here confin'd by you
Or sent to Naples. Let me not,   5
Since I have my dukedom got
And pardon'd the deceiver, dwell
In this bare island by your spell,
But release me from my bands
With the help of your good hands!   10
Gentle breath of yours my sails
Must fill or else my project fails,
Which was to please. Now I want
Spirits to enforce, art to enchant,
And my ending is despair   15
Unless I be reliev'd by prayer
Which pierces so that it assaults
Mercy itself and frees all faults.
    As you from crimes would pardon'd be,   19
    Let your indulgence set me free.   *Exit.*

NOTES

Act I, Scene 1

[The Actors' Names] Based upon the list of characters appended to the Folio text of the play.

councilor The Folio (cited throughout as F) prints *councellor;* the modern 'councilor,' a member of a council, was earlier spelled 'counselor.'

Act I F divides this play into acts and scenes throughout.

3 Good Answering the Boatswain's question, the Master tells him to take heart (be of 'good cheer'). Cf. *cheerly* in l. 5 and 'Cheerly, good hearts' in l. 27. F's punctuation (colons after *Good* and *mariners*) suggests that the meaning is not 'good fellow,' as in l. 15 below, where F has no punctuation after *good.*

7–8 Blow . . . enough A bravado taunt to the wind: 'Blow until you burst your belly, so long as we have sea room enough!' Cf. *Pericles,* III.1.44.

16 cares Variant plural form of verb. Instances of seemingly singular verb and plural subject, as well as many other constructions now considered to be grammatical lapses, are common in Shakespeare and illustrate the fluidity of Elizabethan grammar. That they are not compositor's errors is evidenced by their frequent occurrence in manuscripts.

35 Down . . . topmast For a discussion of this and other nautical expressions consult the Furness Variorum Edition. Shakespeare uses these terms accurately and precisely.

50 ahold This may be a variant of *a-hull,* 'hove-to' (or a printer's error for *a-holl*). See discussion by H. B. Allen, *MLN,* 52 (1937), 96–100, cited in Arden ed. (1954), p. 7.

52–66 These lines are often arranged by editors as blank verse.

53 must . . . cold A euphemism for 'must we die?' Some editors insist that here the Boatswain drinks from a bottle, but there is no textual evidence that Antonio's charge in l. 58 is just.

59 washing . . . tides Pirates were hanged at low-water level in the Thames and left until three tides had washed over their bodies.

Act I, Scene 2

19 more better Double comparative for emphasis, common in Shakespeare and other Elizabethan writers.

24 magic garment The cloak which invests Prospero with power over the elements and humans.

29 soil F *soule*, but cf. ll. 29–31 with ll. 217–18 below, and in II.1.63–106. The alternative is to keep *soule*, follow it with a dash, and assume an anacoluthon.

30 hair A possible pun on *hair—heir*. Cf. the talk of Alonso's loss of a daughter and son in II.1.71–115, especially ll. 113–15. Fathers and heirs are much on Prospero's mind; see above, ll. 19–21; below, ll. 54 ff., especially l. 58.

59 And princess So F. Most editors emend to 'A princess,' but the F text is syntactically satisfactory.

81 trash for overtopping To trash was to check a hound with a long weight. To overtop was to run ahead of the pack.

91–2 With . . . rate I.e. 'with that which, save that it kept me in retirement from the world and my duties, surpassed in value everything the world rates highly.'

97 lorded By construing this as an intransitive verb (with OED authority) we may retain the F full stop after *exact* in l. 99. The alternative is to change the preceding or following full stop to a comma and construe *lorded* as a past participle (so OED on this passage): 'he being thus made a lord.'

99–102 Like . . . lie I.e. 'like one who, having to make his lie credible by frequently repeating it, has come to believe it himself and so made a sinner of his memory.'

169 Now I arise Prospero may have suited the action to the word, though in that case the clause is unnecessary. More probably he refers to the change in his fortune; cf. below, ll. 178–9, 181.

173 princess I.e. 'than any other princess can have made for her.' The word may have been 'princesses' (nouns ending in s were often identical in singular and plural). A third possibility is 'princes.' See Helge Kökeritz, *Shakespeare's Pronunciation* (New Haven, 1953), p. 318.

181–2 A reference to the astrological belief that the position of the stars at the time of an action may determine its outcome.

186 **canst not choose** Having resumed his magic mantle, Prospero has 'charmed' his daughter.

229 **still-vex'd Bermoothes** The only time in the play that the Bermudas are mentioned, in spite of the fact that accounts of a wreck in 1609 off the coast of these traditionally stormy isles appear to be among the sources of the play. See Appendix B.

248 **Told thee . . . made thee** Inclusion of the second *thee* distorts the rhythm of the line to such an extent that we may safely assume it to be a copyist's or compositor's error caused by the two preceding phrases 'done thee' and 'Told thee.'

269 **blue-ey'd** Blue veins in the eyelids were thought to be a symptom of pregnancy. Cf. *The Duchess of Malfi*, II.1.67.

273 **earthy** Ariel, a spirit of the air, could not perform deeds partaking wholly of the nature of earth. Each of the four elements —earth, air, fire, and water—was thought to have its own spirits.

334 **strok'st** For the loss of the past tense ending in such consonant clusters see Kökeritz, *Shakespeare's Pronunciation*, p. 303.

339 **place.** This may be plural. See note on l. 173 above.

352–63 Most editors assign this speech to Prospero, who is a likely candidate, but cf. II.2.141–2. The kindness and the pity are as characteristic of Miranda as of Prospero.

376–86 The song may have been sung to a dance of sea nymphs, hence the reference to sands and waves. The curtsey and kiss were the salutations at the beginning of the dance. F is not clear concerning the lineation of the burden, which has been here slightly altered.

438 **his brave son** This character does not appear in the play. Since F has a comma after *son, his* could refer to the king of Naples were it not for the inescapable fact that Ferdinand could not call himself *brave*.

469 **My . . . tutor** In Shakespeare's day the conception was strong that for a harmonious society everything must find and retain its appointed function. For examples of this homily of the head and foot see Arden ed., p. 40.

Act II, Scene 1

16–20 The obvious pun *dollar—dolour* relies on two meanings of 'entertain': to occupy the attention of, and to provide with food and drink.

33 A laughter 'The whole number of eggs laid by a fowl before she is ready to sit' (OED), with an obvious quibble on the common meaning of *laughter*.

36-7 Editors usually reassign l. 36 to Antonio and l. 37 to Sebastian. The problem may also be resolved by assuming that *you're* is a mistake for *you've*, the loser having to laugh (to cackle like a fowl who has just laid an egg?); or that Sebastian, unable to contain himself, laughed first, and Antonio sarcastically reproved him by pretending he had won.

65 glosses Probably not a mistake for the singular, as many editors believe, but plural because of the plural *garments*—as one might say, 'Gentlemen, put on your hats,' rather than 'hat.'

80 Widow Dido Dido is a character in Virgil's *Aeneid*. Gonzalo may have pronounced *Dido* to rhyme with *Widow* and thus aroused Antonio's scorn, increased by Gonzalo's assertion of the continuity of Carthage and the modern Tunis. Tunis is another city, near the site of ancient Carthage.

107 fish'd for The word *sort* was groped for and well chosen, since (Antonio implies) the doublet is not so fresh as Gonzalo believes; *fish'd* suggests the brine from which Gonzalo has recently pulled himself. A *sort* was a group of things, a gathering, hence possibly a catch of fish.

146 Fowl Pun on *fowl—foul*, and possibly to be associated with 'fool'; see Kökeritz, *Shakespeare's Pronunciation*, pp. 75, 109, 149. The jest of *fowl—foul* lies in the fact that Gonzalo has been called an 'old cock' (l. 30, above; cf. note to l. 33.)

151-73 From Florio's translation of Montaigne, bk. I, ch. 30. See Appendix B, below. Gonzalo is not so serious as the ill-natured Sebastian and Antonio pretend—he is attempting both to divert Alonso from the subject of his grief and to bait Sebastian and Antonio; see ll. 176-9, below.

173 'Save In 1606 an act was passed prohibiting the jesting use of the name of God on the stage. The omission of 'God' in this line may have been due to this prohibition.

187 sphere According to the Ptolemaic conception of the universe there were seven planets revolving about the earth, each in its own sphere. The moon's sphere was closest to the earth.

189 go a-batfowling Hunt birds at night with long clubs (bats). The birds were roused from their sleep in low trees and knocked down as they flew about bewilderedly. Gonzalo is the bird they are knocking down; cf. above, ll. 30, 146, and note to l. 33.

199–202 The lineation has been slightly altered from F.

242 hope Sebastian uses the word to mean 'expectation'; Antonio adds the meaning 'desire' (Kittredge).

257–8 what . . . discharge What happens in the future will depend on how we discharge our duty to make you king.

Act III, Scene 1

15 Most . . . it Elliptical construction: 'when I am most busy I seem least busy, because I think these sweet thoughts of Miranda.' It is a summarizing conclusion to the whole speech.

32 visitation Play on the obvious meaning of the word and its other meaning of bubonic plague, which was thought to be a visitation of the wrath of God on sinful man.

59–63 The Arden ed. (p. 75) suggests a very satisfying rearrangement of these lines which eliminates the metrical irregularities.

Act III, Scene 2

132 picture of No-body A printer named John Trundle used a picture of a man without a body as the sign of his shop. In 1606 he sold a play called *No-body and Some-body*, the title page of which bears a picture of this sign (Var. Ed.).

Act III, Scene 3

17SD Prosper on the top Prospero appears on the upper stage or acting space, looking down upon the action. In F ll. 18–19 are placed after the SD *Enter . . . depart. Banket* was a common spelling of 'banquet' (a light supper) and indicates the pronunciation.

96

23 phoenix Mythical bird thought to be unique and endowed with the ability to immolate itself and rise from its own ashes.

48 putter . . . one In the days when travel to a foreign country was an exceedingly hazardous undertaking, it was the custom of travelers to lay wagers against their safe return, the odds being five to one in favor of the traveler.

55 surfeited Should probably be read *surfeit*, an alternative past participle. Note also other probable contractions in this speech: *being* (monosyllable), *I have* ('I've'), and *even* ('e'en').

Act IV, Scene 1

3 third A good share. Kittredge's conjecture cannot be bettered: Since life consists of past, present, and future, and since Prospero lives for his daughter (l. 4), in a sense she is his future, i.e. one-third of his life. In l. 4 *Or* has the effect of 'Or in other words.'

27 worser genius It was thought that two spirits, a good and a bad, fought for control of each man.

64 pioned and twilled Probably 'trenched' (cf. 'pioner' and 'pioneer,' a digger of trenches) and 'grained' (like twill cloth, e.g.) from the winter weather. A contrast is drawn between the banks of a river in early spring and the same banks covered with April verdure.

72SD Juno . . . descend This SD from F is often omitted, on the ground that Juno does not enter until l. 102, but there seems no good reason to doubt the authority of F. From the hints of ll. 37, 74, and 93 it seems likely that a stage machine lowered her sufficiently to provide the spectacle of a flying chariot moving across the stage. She could have been deposited at the proper time to take her entrance cue.

130 land This may be 'laund,' a glade, a later form of which is the modern 'lawn.' Cf. *3 Henry VI*, III.1.2.

193 line Probably a lime or linden tree (cf. 'line grove' below, V.1.10; and there is good authority elsewhere). The alternative is a clothes line.

222 O . . . peer 'In *Oth.*, II.iii.92, are two stanzas of a ballad

97

printed in Percy's *Reliques*, entitled "Take thy old cloak about thee"; one of these is as follows: "King Stephen was a worthy peere,/His breeches cost him but a crowne,/ He held them sixpence all too deere;/ Therefore he called the taylor Lowne." Hence Trinculo's remark, "What a wardrobe" ' (Arden ed., p. 107).

235–8 **Mistress . . . bald jerkin** The meaning of this passage is largely dependent on the stage business, which was very likely on the vulgar side. It is necessary to remember that 'under the line,' meaning 'below the equator' (a fitting nautical term in Stephano's mouth) meant also 'under the lime tree' (see note above on l. 193). Although the jerkin could have been a hair or fur jerkin, the point of the jest of ll. 237–8 remains obscure unless we remember that 'loin' and 'line' were homonyms (Kökeritz, *Shakespeare's Pronunciation*, p. 125). The drunken Stephano lifts the jerkin off the line (tree) and passes it between his legs (under the line—loin) with an indecent motion (jerkin'). Losing the hair was one of the supposed effects of syphilis (cf. *Measure for Measure*, I.2.34–5), hence the *bald* (with double-entendre) jerkin afterward.

239 **we . . . level** Trinculo adds to the puns on *line:* 'by line and level' means by mason's plumb line and level, hence 'by rule,' 'skillfully.' But in view of the preceding business and the proximity of the lime tree, a pun on *steal—stale* is almost inevitable. To stale was to urinate (said of horses, dogs, etc.). The word is ironic in the light of *stale* in l. 187 above.

245 **lime** Still another play on line-linden-lime tree. The reference is to the catching of birds by placing sticky lime on trees.

Act V, Scene 1

21–4 If you, who are composed of nothing but air, have been able to feel some compassion for their troubled state, shall not I, human like themselves and able to experience emotion fully as sharply, be moved more than you to behave as a human and take pity on them?

174–5 **Yes . . . play** I agree that you would not cheat, and even if you disputed over twenty kingdoms (instead of this insignificant game of chess), I would still insist you would not cheat.

236 **our trim** An important aspect of the clothes imagery in this play is the fact that no one's clothes sustained as much as a blemish, with the exception of Stephano's and Trinculo's. Here the Boatswain is using a nautical term to express the idea.

267 **badges** Either the insignia of Prospero attached to the shoulders of the coats, as was customary on the clothing of retainers, or, figuratively, the stolen coats themselves as badges of their guilt.

APPENDIX A

Text and Date

The earliest published text of *The Tempest* is in the First Folio, 1623. It is the first play in that volume and one of the most painstakingly printed: only a handful of indisputable typographical errors can be found, the verse lineation is on the whole well preserved, the stage directions are remarkably full, and the punctuation is admirably consistent.

In spite of the obvious care taken with punctuation by the first editors, it has been felt necessary to assist the modern reader by converting the pointing entirely to present-day usage. For example, colons in the Folio text appear in the present edition as colons, semicolons, exclamation points, dashes, or periods, though usually the colon in the original has the force of the modern exclamation point, which indeed in almost every instance would have been the mark substituted if other considerations had not dictated variety.

Few liberties have been taken with the text. These few have been recorded in the glosses and notes, with the exception of a slight shift in position of a stage direction here and there, as in I.1.38–9; in the Folio this direction follows line 36. Whenever anything has been added to the text, it has been placed within square brackets.

Throughout the play, though most frequently in Act I, are defective lines (for instance I.2.159, 195, 235, 253, 269; II.1.259, 312; IV.1.12; V.1.61). These lines—short by one, two, or three metrical feet—have sometimes been used as evidence for a theory that Act I as it now stands is a cut version, the cuts having been made at the places where the faulty lines occur. In the absence of bibliographical corroboration, however, there seems no need to believe that the extant version is not as Shakespeare wrote it, particularly since irregular lines can be found in other Shakespearean plays, and in *The Tempest* the short lines occur at places where a slight pause assists both the sense and the rhythm.

It should also be noted that a few verse lines have been rearranged slightly to make the length of each more regular; see I.2.302–5, 362–3; II.1.196–7, 198–202. A few lines here printed as verse are probably prose (for example II.1.205–6); a few other lines set as verse in the Folio now appear as prose (for example II.1.16–17); and Caliban's speech in II.2.170–5 has been set as verse but appears as prose in the Folio.

From the very slight bibliographical evidence available it is not possible to do more than guess at the form of the copy supplied the printer of the Folio. It could well have been a prompt copy that had been carefully edited by one or another member of the acting company. Its division into acts and scenes and the inclusion of a list of actors, as well as the full stage directions and consistent punctuation mentioned above, may indicate merely that the editors wanted the first play in their volume to make a good impression. Almost the only mark of carelessness that one can note, in fact, is the circumstance that some obvious prose lines are set as verse and some verse as prose. Here it is important to observe, however, that for the actor a few lines or even passages of verse set as prose, or vice versa, would surely have made no difference in his reading of those lines, the important thing in delivery being the sense of rhythm of the complete speech and scene. This must have been doubly true on the Shakespearean stage, where, from all we can learn, the actor's delivery was rapid. If anything, such mistakes in lineation argue that the play was set from playhouse prompt copy.

In any event Shakespeare wrote it at least twelve years before it was printed, for the accounts of the Office of Revels contain a note that it was presented on Hallowmas night (November 1), 1611. There is some negative evidence that it was not being played during the summer of 1611, and one of the sources Shakespeare made use of could not have been seen by him before late 1610. Thus the best inference that can be drawn concerning the date of composition is sometime between October 1610 and October 1611. Apart from collaboration in *Henry VIII* and *Two Noble Kinsmen*, it was probably Shakespeare's last effort.

APPENDIX B

Sources

The true source of *The Tempest* is Shakespeare's experience in coming to terms with life. The symbols which permeate it lie so deep and so near to the heart of humanity that even if a closely parallel play or narrative were to be unearthed—and this hypothesis is dubious in the extreme—it could only in a very limited sense be called a source. The billowing themes of Shakespeare's tragedies, the nuances of the comedies, the moral philosophy that threads its way through the histories—all are here and thoroughly Shakespearean and so worked into the matrix of the play that one can believe it the full and natural expression of what was most meaningful to Shakespeare in life.

This is not to call *The Tempest* a conscious farewell to a career. It is highly ironical that the one speech in the play that really sounds as though Shakespeare were taking leave of the stage is one of the few which derive from earlier works: Prospero's conjuring of the spirits in V.1.33–57 comes from Obid's *Metamorphoses* VII.192–219—partly from the original Latin, partly from Arthur Golding's English translation (many editions after 1567). This is typical of the so-called sources of the play—a line here or there, at the most a few brief passages garnered from well-known works.

Two of the most popular works at the time the play was being written—and together with a manuscript letter in circulation among the playwright's friends perhaps the origin of his initial inspiration—were concerned with a highly romantic and for the religious a nearly miraculous wreck off the Bermudas in July 1609. For several years before, public interest in the new Virginia colony in America had been running high. When a fleet of nine ships under the command of Sir George Somers (or Summers) put to sea on June 2, 1609, considerable fanfare and putting of pen to paper accompanied the great setting forth.

Nothing was heard in England about the results of the voyage (except that one of the ships was supposed lost) until the governor of Virginia, who had sailed with the fleet, returned in 1610. It then became known that off the coast of the 'still-vex'd Bermoothes' (Shakespeare uses the common spelling-equivalent of the Spanish *Bermudez*) the flagship had run into a hurricane and having been forced to enter a sheltered cove was there run aground. No lives had been lost, and the implications of this as they concerned the intrepid colonizers of a savage land were not missed by the morally minded Elizabethans. Among the pamphlets which appeared in 1610 were two containing accounts of the wreck and subsequent survival of the voyagers, both sufficiently close to Shakespeare's play to make it seem almost certain he knew of them: Sylvester Jourdain's *Discovery of the Barmudas* (facsimile by J. Q. Adams, New York, 1940) and the Council of Virginia's *True Declaration of the State of the Colonie in Virginia* (ed. Peter Force as vol. *3* of *Tracts and Other Papers*, Washington, 1844).

Even more than to these 'Bermuda pamphlets' is Shakespeare indebted to a letter written by one William Strachey and brought to England shortly after July 15, 1610. Although this letter was not published (so far as is known) until 1625, when it appeared as 'A True Reportory of the Wracke' in *Purchas His Pilgrimes* (vol. *19* of the Glasgow ed., 1906), Leslie Hotson has demonstrated that it was being circulated among friends of Shakespeare who could very easily have shown it to him (*I, William Shakespeare*, London, 1937). The whole of the first scene of *The Tempest* seems to derive from Strachey's account, as do I.2.195–205, much of II.1, the appearance of the banquet in III, and a few more scattered passages.

The other works to which Shakespeare might have given acknowledgment may be quickly disposed of. Gonzalo's references in III.3.44–7 to the dewlapped mountaineers and men with heads in their breasts are straight from the most widely read adventure book of the period: the *Travels of Sir John Mandeville*, III.3. Gonzalo's disquisition on the ideal commonwealth in II.1.149–69 is derived from Montaigne's 'Of Cannibals,' translated by John Florio, 1603. The name 'Setebos' probably stems from Robert Eden's *History of Travaile*, 1577, in which it is claimed that the Patagonians have a 'great devil' called this. The origin of

'Caliban' cannot be pinned down. It may be simply an anagram of 'can[n]ibal' or it may be related to *cauliban*, a gypsy word for blackness, though Virgil and Pliny both mention savages named 'Chalybeates.' The name 'Prospero' occurs in William Thomas' *The Historie of Italie*, 1549.

All other of the 'sources' which at one time or another have been put forth as the primary source are little more than analogues. Thus certain *scenari* of the Italian commedia dell' arte have points of resemblance with the plot of *The Tempest;* the last word on these may not yet have been said. A play by the German Jakob Ayrer (died 1605) called, in translation, *The Beautiful Sidea*, was formerly hailed by the Germans as the archetype, but anyone who takes the trouble to read it will come to the conclusion that only two salient details lend any point whatever to the supposed connection: (1) a prince is held in thrall by the beautiful Sidea and made to carry logs for her, and (2) his sword is charmed, so that he cannot use it. Although these coincidences are interesting, they do not mean that either play necessarily descends from the other. At the same time the possibility of a lost *tertium quid* cannot be dismissed.

In sum, so far as research can discover, Shakespeare borrowed remarkably little. Research will go on, for it is in the nature of source hunters to believe that by turning pages they will eventually upset all vested notions. Sometimes they are remarkably successful; yet for *The Tempest*, it seems safe to prophesy, the results will hardly be worth the effort. The true sources are the three dozen plays of Shakespeare which preceded it, together with the feelings, deeper than ever plummet sounded, of a man who considered life gravely and wrote it down incomparably.

APPENDIX C

Reading List

ROBERT R. CAWLEY, 'Shakspere's Use of the Voyagers in *The Tempest,*' *PMLA, 41* (1926), 688–726.

E. K. CHAMBERS, 'The Integrity of *The Tempest,*' *RES, 1* (1925), 129–50.

BONAMY DOBRÉE, '*The Tempest,*' *Essays and Studies, 5* (1952), 13–25.

A. H. GILBERT, 'The *Tempest* Parallelism in Characters and Situations,' *JEGP, 14* (1915), 63–74.

J. E. HANKINS, 'Caliban the Bestial Man,' *PMLA, 62* (1947), 793–801.

FRANK KERMODE, ed., *The Tempest,* Arden ed., London, 1954.

HELGE KÖKERITZ, *Shakespeare's Pronunciation,* New Haven, 1953.

HELGE KÖKERITZ and CHARLES T. PROUTY, eds., *Mr. William Shakespeares Comedies, Histories, & Tragedies,* Facsimile of First Folio, New Haven, 1954.

DONALD A. STAUFFER, *Shakespeare's World of Images,* New York, 1949.

DEREK A. TRAVERSI, '*The Tempest,*' *Scrutiny, 16* (1949), 127–57.

J. DOVER WILSON, ed., *The Tempest,* New Shakespeare ed., Cambridge, 1921.